Should You Start a Business or Not?

Critical Considerations and Success Tips

A Practical Guide for Your Business Entry Decision

CHARLIE VICTOR

Impisi™

Impisi™ Media LLC
Small Business Series

Should You Start a Business or Not?

A Practical Guide for Your Business Entry Decision

CHARLIE VICTOR

Impisi™ Media LLC

ISBN:978-1-965722-03-9 (eBook)
ISBN:978-1-965722-04-6 (Paperback)

The case studies in this book are based on real-life experiences. To protect privacy, names, locations, and identifying details have been changed or omitted. Any resemblance to persons, businesses, or places beyond the intended examples is coincidental. The lessons and insights are genuine and provide practical guidance to readers on their entrepreneurial journey.

Book design by Ciska Venter.

First printing edition 2024.

Published by Impisi™ Media LLC in the United States of America.
5830 E 2ND ST, STE 7000, CASPER, WY 82609
+1 (307) 275 8745
Visit our website www.impisimedia.com
Impisi™ is subject to a trademark application by Impisi Media LLC.

Contents

Contents

"You always do what you want to do. This is true with every act. You may say that you had to do something, or that you were forced to, but actually, whatever you do, you do by choice. Only you have the power to choose for yourself" – W. Clement Stone

Every decision is a choice. Every choice is a decision. Whether freely or through compulsion, there is always an option. And choices are destiny makers.

Introduction

"Entrepreneurship is living a few years of your life like most people won't, so that you can spend the rest of your life like most people can't" — Austin Netzley

Purpose of the Book

E ntrepreneurship often seems glamorous and exciting, with stories of overnight successes and thriving businesses. However, the reality is different. The early days of searching, researching, and soul-searching can be lonely and difficult. These times are often filled with uncertainty and doubt.

This book aims to be your guide through these challenging times. It seeks to inform you about the essentials of starting and running a business. The book will help clarify your thoughts and provide a structured approach to decision-making. It offers practical advice and points you toward additional resources when you need more in-depth knowledge. The book aims to help you build a solid foundation for your entrepreneurial journey by offering this support.

Starting a business is risky, but this book aims to turn that risk into a calculated one. By giving new entrepreneurs the necessary knowledge, this book helps reduce uncertainty and guesswork.

Making informed decisions based on well-researched information helps to ease the doubts and anxieties of starting a new venture. The goal is to arm you with tools to transform potential pitfalls into manageable challenges.

This book is designed to give you the confidence to take those first steps toward entrepreneurship. It provides a foundation of knowledge to help you navigate the complexities and challenges you will face. The goal is not to eliminate risk—impossible in business—but to help you manage and mitigate it effectively. Knowing what to expect and being prepared for various scenarios can significantly impact your entrepreneurial experience.

The book aims to inspire and motivate you in addition to practical advice. The entrepreneurial journey is a marathon, not a sprint, so keeping your motivation and enthusiasm high is crucial. Throughout the book, you will find real-life examples, case studies, and anecdotes from successful entrepreneurs. These stories are meant to inspire you and show that, with the right mindset and tools, you can overcome challenges and achieve your business goals. Seeing how others have navigated similar paths can provide invaluable insights and encouragement.

Finally, this book emphasizes continuous learning and adaptation. The business landscape constantly changes, so staying updated with the latest trends, technologies, and best practices is essential. This book encourages a mindset of lifelong learning. You can keep your business relevant and competitive by embracing change and being open to new ideas.

By the end of this book, you will have the knowledge and the confidence to start your entrepreneurial journey. You will be equipped with the tools and insights needed to turn your business ideas into reality, understanding the risks involved and how to manage them effectively. The journey will still have challenges, but you will be better prepared to face them head-on.

How to Use This Book

To get the most from this book, consider these approaches. First, read it cover to cover. This comprehensive approach will give you a solid foundation and a broad understanding of the entrepreneurial landscape. You'll gain insights into various aspects of starting and running a business, preparing you for the journey ahead. Immersing yourself fully in the content ensures you grasp the big picture and the interconnectedness of various business aspects.

Focus on relevant chapters if you have specific areas of interest or immediate needs. This targeted approach lets you address particular questions or challenges you're currently facing. For example, if you're interested in different business structures, go straight to that section for an in-depth look. Tailoring your reading to your immediate needs can make learning more efficient and relevant.

This book is a versatile resource. Combine it with other materials to enhance your learning experience. Use the additional readings (Appendix B: Resources) and references (Appendix C: Glossary) to deepen your understanding. This ensures you have a well-rounded perspective and comprehensive knowledge. You can develop a more nuanced understanding of the topics by integrating various sources.

As you read, make notes of your preferences, decisions, and ideas. This practice helps reinforce what you've learned and allows you to personalize the content. Use these notes to create a roadmap tailored to your unique situation, which will be a valuable tool as you progress. Writing down your thoughts and reflections can also help clarify your thinking and solidify your plans.

Develop a personalized action plan based on the book's insights and strategies. This proactive approach helps you implement the knowledge you gain and track your progress. Refer to your action plan to stay focused as you encounter new challenges and opportunities. An action plan provides a clear path forward and can help keep you accountable for your goals.

Refer to Appendix A for a suggested action plan based on this book.

Highlight important information and bookmark key passages for future reference. This practice makes it easier to revisit crucial concepts and strategies. Entrepreneurship is dynamic, and having quick access to essential information will be invaluable as you adapt to new circumstances and refine your plan. Keeping key points handy ensures you can quickly refresh your memory when needed.

Remember, this book is not just a one-time read. Think of it as a reference guide you can return to whenever you need guidance or a refresher. As your business grows and evolves, the information and advice will remain relevant, helping you navigate new challenges and seize new opportunities. The principles and strategies outlined in this book are designed to be timeless, offering value at every stage of your entrepreneurial journey.

By following these guidelines, you can maximize the benefits of this book and make it a practical tool in your path to successful entrepreneurship. Use it as a companion on your journey, providing the knowledge, strategies, and inspiration to turn your business dreams into reality.

Chapter 1
Reasons to Go into Business

"The best reason to start an organization is to make meaning; to create a product or service to make the world a better place" — *Guy Kawasaki*

Overview

Before exploring the diverse types of businesses you can start, we must delve into why one would choose to embark on this journey.

Understanding the reasons behind starting a business is crucial. These motivations shape your approach, influence your decisions, and sustain you through challenges. Whether it's the allure of financial freedom or the pursuit of a personal passion, your 'why' serves as a compass, guiding you toward success.

This chapter will cover seven reasons to start a business. First, the desire for independence drives many to seek control over their destinies, free from the constraints of traditional employment. Financial goals are another powerful motivator, as entrepreneurship offers the potential for significant economic rewards. Passion and interest often ignite the enterprising spirit, turning hobbies into thriving enterprises. Recognizing a market opportunity can also spark the decision to start a business, as can unforeseen personal circumstances that necessitate a career shift. For some, the chance to make a social impact is a key driver, while others are drawn to entrepreneurship's lifestyle benefits.

Understanding these reasons can help you better align your motivations with your business goals, ensuring a more fulfilling entrepreneurial journey.

Desire for Independence

Independence is a deeply rooted desire for many individuals. It is the freedom to make one's own choices, the ability to shape one's destiny, and the autonomy to live life on one's terms. For some, this longing for independence is a philosophical journey, a quest to break free from the constraints imposed by external forces.

Independence means liberation from the traditional 9-to-5 grind, from reporting to a boss, and from being tethered to a rigid corporate structure. It is a pursuit of self-governance, where one's path is self-determined rather than dictated by others.

In an entrepreneur's day-to-day life, this independence can take many forms. It means setting your schedule and deciding where and when to work. It manifests in the freedom to make pivotal decisions without waiting for approval from a boss.

An entrepreneur has the liberty to shape the company's culture, from its vision and mission down to the dress code. This control extends to the ability to implement changes swiftly, adapting to market conditions or personal preferences without bureaucratic delays. Independence allows entrepreneurs to create a work environment that aligns with their values and vision, fostering a sense of ownership and pride.

There are numerous benefits to achieving independence in business. Having control over the business culture means that every aspect, from the company's core values to its daily operations, can reflect the founder's ideals. Entrepreneurs can establish a unique identity for their business that resonates with their personal beliefs and attracts like-minded employees and customers.

The ability to make decisions autonomously allows for quick responses to opportunities or challenges, enabling the business to remain agile and competitive. A flexible schedule is another significant advantage, providing the opportunity to balance work with personal commitments and passions. This flexibility can lead to a more fulfilling and balanced life, where work complements rather than conflicts with individual goals.

However, the quest for independence has its challenges. Full responsibility for the business means bearing the weight of every decision, success, and failure. This can lead to significant stress, especially in times of uncertainty or difficulty. As much as independence can allow a flexible work schedule, the time commitment needed to run a business is substantial, often demanding long hours and sacrificing personal time.

Achieving a work-life balance can be particularly challenging, as the lines between professional and personal life blur. Depending on the size of the business, the entrepreneur might find themselves in a lonely position, lacking a management team to share the burden of decision-making and strategic planning. This isolation can be daunting, as the responsibility for every aspect of the business rests solely on their shoulders.

Moreover, some entrepreneurs are so bent on independence that they are willing to sacrifice growth opportunities or profitability to be the king of their castle. This desire for total control can sometimes hinder the business's potential to scale or attract investment, as external input and collaboration are often necessary for substantial growth.

While keeping complete control can ensure that the business remains true to the founder's vision, it can also limit the company's ability to adapt and expand in a competitive market. Entrepreneurs must carefully weigh the benefits of independence against the potential trade-offs in growth and profitability.

In summary, the desire for independence drives many to entrepreneurship, offering a path to autonomy and self-determination. The freedom to shape one's destiny is a powerful motivator, bringing substantial rewards and significant challenges. By understanding the implications of this independence, entrepreneurs can better prepare for the journey ahead, balancing the benefits of autonomy with the realities of total responsibility.

Financial Goals

Financial goals are a significant driving force for many entrepreneurs. In fact, many would argue that it is the only reason for going into business. Why would anyone accept the challenges unless they were rewarded by profit? If not for profit, business would just be working for a boss called Me.

These goals can vary widely, ranging from earning a livable income that comfortably supports one's lifestyle to achieving sufficient wealth for an early retirement. Some entrepreneurs aim to leave a financial legacy for their families, while others pursue outright wealth and financial independence.

For instance, a freelance graphic designer might aim to earn enough to pay their bills and maintain a comfortable home office, enjoying a modest but stable lifestyle. On the other end of the spectrum, a tech start-up founder might aspire to build a company valued in the millions, enabling them to sell the business, travel extensively, invest in other innovative projects, and live with complete financial freedom.

Wealth is a relative concept and does not mean the same thing to everyone. What one person considers financial success may differ vastly from another's definition. Some might see wealth as having millions in the bank, while others might define it as having the financial stability to live life on their terms without worry.

The desire for wealth and financial freedom is not unethical or wrong; it is a personal goal unique to everyone. Pursuing financial goals is about achieving a sense of security and fulfillment that aligns with one's values and aspirations.

Having clear financial goals offers several advantages. It provides a sense of direction and purpose, helping entrepreneurs make informed decisions and set priorities. Clear goals enable better financial planning, ensuring that resources are allocated efficiently to achieve desired outcomes. With defined targets, entrepreneurs can measure their progress, celebrate milestones, and adjust strategies as needed.

However, achieving these goals requires personal investment, both in terms of time and money. Entrepreneurs must be prepared to commit their resources to realize their financial aspirations.

The real-life financial landscape of businesses, especially start-ups, can be challenging. Actual results often differ significantly from initial goals, usually skewing towards the negative. Many start-ups face financial difficulties, with inconsistent income and the risk of monetary loss.

Entrepreneurs may find themselves in debt as they invest heavily in their businesses, hoping for future returns. The pressure to achieve financial goals can lead to stress and anxiety, as the path to success is fraught with uncertainty and obstacles. It's important to acknowledge that the road to financial success is rarely smooth and requires resilience and adaptability.

Financial goals often evolve. An entrepreneur might initially seek to replace their previous salary but, as their business grows and they become more experienced, aim for higher profits or expansion into new markets. This dynamic nature of financial goals requires continuous reassessment and flexibility. Entrepreneurs must remain adaptable and ready to pivot their strategies as their financial landscape changes.

Despite these challenges, the balance of risk and reward is a fundamental aspect of entrepreneurship. The possibility of significant rewards counters the potential for financial loss. Entrepreneurs have the freedom to choose how they manage this balance, tailoring their approach to their risk tolerance and financial goals. Understanding and accepting the inherent risks enables them to navigate the economic landscape more effectively, making strategic decisions that align with their long-term goals.

In summary, financial goals are a core motivator for many entrepreneurs, shaping their actions and strategies. While the pursuit of financial success comes with challenges and risks, it also offers the potential for substantial rewards. By setting clear financial goals and understanding the realities of the business landscape, entrepreneurs can balance ambition with pragmatism.

Interest, Passion, and Talent

While passion and interest are often closely related, they are not identical.

Interest is a broader term, often associated with an early stage of attraction to a subject or activity. It's the curiosity that sparks initial engagement and exploration. Interest might lead someone to learn more about a particular field, dabble in related activities, or follow trends and news within that area. It's a significant starting point but tends to be more superficial and fleeting than passion.

Passion, on the other hand, is a more profound enthusiasm that borders on commitment. It's a stronger emotion than interest, closely linked to personal drive and motivation. Passion is what keeps someone engaged and motivated through challenges and setbacks. It involves a sense of purpose and dedication that sustains long-term effort. Passionate individuals often go above and beyond, investing time, energy, and resources into their pursuits with unwavering commitment.

In the context of starting a business, interest is a good starting point, but more is likely needed to sustain the venture over the long term. Interest might get you to explore the idea of entrepreneurship, but it's a passion that will provide the motivation and determination required to overcome obstacles and persist through tough times. Passion drives the continuous effort needed to build and grow a business, turning challenges into opportunities and keeping the entrepreneur focused on their vision.

However, there are nuances to this dynamic. Interest can turn into passion as one delves deeper into a subject and finds greater meaning and satisfaction in it. Conversely, even the strongest passion can wane over time, especially if faced with prolonged challenges, burnout, or shifting personal priorities. Understanding these nuances is crucial for entrepreneurs, as it helps them recognize when they need to reignite their passion or pivot to keep their drive.

Adding a third aspect to this discussion, talent is another critical factor. Talent refers to a natural aptitude or skill in a particular area. Operating within your talent spectrum means using your innate strengths, which can significantly impact your chances of success.

Talent is often related to interest, as people are generally drawn to activities in which they excel. It also relates to passion, as excelling in a field can deepen one's enthusiasm and commitment.

Recognizing and harnessing your talent can lead to more efficient and effective work. For instance, an entrepreneur with a talent for networking and building relationships may find securing partnerships, clients, and resources easier. This natural skill can turn into a significant business advantage, allowing for growth and expansion that might be more challenging for someone without this talent. Additionally, working within your talent spectrum can lead to greater job satisfaction and fulfillment, as tasks feel less like work and more like a natural extension of your abilities.

Warren Buffett is an excellent example of an entrepreneur who followed his talent instead of passion. Known for his extraordinary talent in investing, Buffett's success is attributed to his exceptional skill in analyzing businesses and making investment decisions, which may have started as an interest but evolved into a passion aligned with his talents. This alignment of talent, interest, and passion has allowed Buffett to achieve remarkable success and sustain his enthusiasm for his work over decades.

Here are three quotes from well-known entrepreneurs about this very discussion we are having. This is something to consider, as it highlights a different aspect each considers important.

"Talent is cheaper than table salt. What separates the talented from the successful is the ability to handle rejection. It's about surrounding yourself with the right people. Are you coachable? Are you willing to learn? Are you willing to work hard?" - Steve Jobs

"I think it's very important to have a deep passion about what you're doing." - Elon Musk

"The most important thing is to enjoy the process. If you're not enjoying it, you're not going to be successful." - Mark Zuckerberg

In summary, while interest is a great starting point, more is needed to sustain a business. Passion provides the necessary drive and commitment to overcome challenges and achieve long-term success. Talent, meanwhile, enhances both interest and passion, providing a foundation of skill and aptitude that can significantly boost an entrepreneur's potential. By understanding and integrating these three aspects—interest, passion, and talent—entrepreneurs can better navigate their journey, aligning their pursuits with their strengths and sustaining their motivation over time.

Market Opportunity

Some entrepreneurs start a business purely because the market opportunity presents itself.

Market opportunity refers to the potential for a new product or service to fulfill unmet customer needs or to offer a better solution than what currently exists. Entrepreneurs identify gaps in the market or emerging trends and assess whether there is a viable opportunity to capitalize on these insights.

Market opportunity can be quantified in several ways. One standard method is through market research, which involves gathering data on consumer behavior, preferences, and spending patterns. This can include surveys, focus groups, and analysis of existing market data.

Additionally, entrepreneurs may look at market size, which shows the total potential sales for a product or service. Growth rate is another crucial factor, as it shows how quickly the market is expanding and whether there is room for new entrants. Competitive analysis helps in understanding the number of existing players and their market share. At the same time, customer segmentation provides insights into specific groups that might be underserved or particularly receptive to a new offering.

Using market opportunity as a reason to start a business has several advantages. One of the most significant benefits is the potential for rapid growth and profitability. When an entrepreneur enters a market with high demand and low competition, there is a greater chance of quickly capturing a substantial market share. This can lead to faster revenue generation and a more significant market presence. Additionally, starting a business based on a clear market opportunity can attract investors and partners, as the potential for return on investment is clearer.

However, even if a substantial market opportunity exists, several aspects must be considered. Market volatility is a critical factor; consumer preferences and market conditions can change rapidly, making it essential to stay adaptable and responsive.

Competition is another primary concern. Even if a market initially appears to have low competition, new entrants can quickly emerge, intensifying the competitive landscape. Market saturation occurs when too many comparable products or services flood the market, making it harder to stand out and attract customers.

Disruptive innovations or technology can also affect market opportunities. Innovations can make existing solutions obsolete or significantly alter customer expectations.

An example of disruptive technology impacting the retail market is the rapid shift towards multichannel retailing. This approach integrates online and offline sales strategies, drastically altering how consumers shop and how retailers operate.

One major disruptor has been the rise of e-commerce platforms and their integration with physical stores. Retailers like Amazon have set new standards with personalized shopping experiences, forcing traditional retailers to adapt quickly to remain competitive. For instance, Home Depot has successfully implemented a multichannel strategy, offering services like "click and collect" and personalized marketing to enhance online and in-store customer engagement.

This example illustrates how quickly a substantial and established market can be disrupted by technology, putting pressure on entrepreneurs to innovate and adapt to maintain market share.

Capturing a meaningful market share requires more than just finding an opportunity; it involves strategic planning, effective marketing, and exceptional customer service. Entrepreneurs must build a strong brand, establish a loyal customer base, and continuously innovate to keep their competitive edge.

In summary, while identifying and capitalizing on market opportunities can be a powerful motivator for starting a business, it requires thorough research and planning. Entrepreneurs must be prepared to navigate market volatility, competition, and potential saturation, and stay agile in the face of disruptive innovations. By understanding these challenges, entrepreneurs can successfully capture and sustain a significant market share, turning opportunities into long-term business success.

Unforeseen Personal Circumstances

Unforeseen personal circumstances refer to the unexpected and often unwelcome events that life throws our way, disrupting our plans and challenging our resilience.

These include situations such as retrenchment, whether fair or not, with or without notice. Other events include becoming physically disabled following a health condition or accident, divorce, the death of a close family member, and poor health. These circumstances can be overwhelming, but they can also present unforeseen opportunities to start a business, either as a choice or a necessity, when no other options are available.

Any of these situations can catalyze entrepreneurship. For some, it might be the only viable option, forcing them to leap into the business world. Despite the hardship, these moments can also bring out the best in people, providing motivation to overcome sudden challenges and create something meaningful.

Starting a business under these circumstances has potential benefits. The motivation to succeed can be powerful, fueled by the desire to overcome adversity. The business can become a source of personal pride and a means to regain control over one's life.

The empathy and support from the community and target market can also provide an emotional and financial boost. Stories of triumph over adversity resonate with people, potentially leading to increased customer loyalty and support.

However, there are also downsides. The unplanned nature of the situation can bring about massive uncertainty and stress, piling pressure onto the entrepreneur already in a challenging situation.

Financial strain is often a major concern, as starting a business typically requires capital, which might be limited following an unforeseen event. Lack of knowledge and experience can also be a barrier, making the journey more challenging.

The emotional toll of dealing with personal crises while trying to set up a business can be overwhelming, requiring a solid support network and resilience.

One real-life example of a successful business that started with little capital after sudden retrenchment is Airbnb. After losing their jobs in 2007, co-founders Brian Chesky and Joe Gebbia rented out air mattresses in their apartment to make ends meet.

The idea took off, addressing a gap in the market for affordable, unique accommodations. With the addition of co-founder Nathan Blecharczyk, Airbnb grew into a global platform connecting travelers with hosts offering everything from spare rooms to entire homes, revolutionizing the hospitality industry.

Naked Divorce was born from the personal pain of Adèle Théron, who experienced the shattering impact of divorce firsthand. Recognizing a void in the market for straightforward, compassionate support, she turned her challenge into a driving force for change.

With unwavering determination, Adèle founded Naked Divorce, a company dedicated to helping others navigate the complexities of divorce with honesty, efficiency, and empathy. Her journey became the blueprint for a business offering a lifeline to those looking to rebuild their lives after heartbreak.

Another inspiring example is the story of Noah Galloway, a U.S. Army veteran who became disabled after losing an arm and a leg in combat. Determined to overcome his physical challenges, Noah turned to fitness and eventually started his career as a personal trainer, motivational speaker, and author. He used his story and experience to gain significant media attention and build a successful brand. Noah's journey proves how personal adversity can lead to a fulfilling and profitable business venture.

In summary, life happens, and unforeseen personal circumstances can disrupt our plans and force us into unexpected paths. While these situations are challenging and stressful, they can also open doors to new opportunities. With determination, support, and resilience, it is possible to turn adversity into a successful business venture.

Social Impact

Social impact refers to the effect an organization has on the well-being of the communities and individuals it interacts with. This involves initiatives that improve lives, such as job creation, community engagement, and contributions to social causes.

Environmental impact, on the other hand, concerns the effect a business has on the planet, including its carbon footprint, resource usage, and waste production. Collectively, these impacts are often referred to as the people/planet impact.

Starting a business with the goal of making a positive people/planet impact can be a valid and compelling reason. In a later chapter, we discuss how non-profit organizations typically deliver these impacts. However, starting a for-profit business to achieve these goals is not only acceptable but is likely to be more effective.

A profit motive ensures that the business stays sustainable and can continue delivering positive impacts over time. Without sufficient profit to re-invest and grow, these impacts cannot be delivered on a continuous basis.

This touches on the broader topic of sustainability, which will be covered later in the series.

Using people/planet impact as a reason to start a business has several advantages. First, it allows entrepreneurs to make a tangible difference in the world. This can lead to strong community support and customer loyalty, as people are more likely to support businesses that align with their values.

Personal fulfillment is another significant benefit, as entrepreneurs can take pride in knowing that their work contributes to the greater good. Additionally, businesses with strong social and environmental missions often leave a legacy, affecting future generations positively.

However, the challenges require careful consideration. Balancing conventional business goals with people/planet goals can be difficult. Too much emphasis on social and environmental goals might lead to financial instability if not managed properly.

Securing funding can be another hurdle, as mainstream financiers typically prioritize profit over impact. A focus on impact can also result in slower growth, as resources are often diverted to social and environmental initiatives rather than expansion.

When there is a prominent people/planet angle to a business, I prefer an outright for-profit model over a non-profit solution.

Private ownership and a profit motive driven by a good entrepreneur can outpace a non-profit led by a competent employee. Sound business planning and decisions should come first, with the impact because of that – not the other way around.

CVS Health exemplifies a for-profit business delivering significant environmental impacts in the healthcare sector. The company has implemented initiatives to reduce its carbon footprint, such as installing solar panels on their stores and distribution centers and promoting energy efficiency across its operations.

In education, 2U Inc. is a for-profit company that partners with leading universities to offer online degree programs. By using technology, 2U expands access to higher education, making it more affordable and accessible to students globally.

One of the most heartwarming examples is John's Crazy Socks. It was born from a father-son dream. John, with Down syndrome, had a passion for colorful socks. Together with his dad, Mark, they turned this love into a thriving business. Beyond selling socks, they created a platform to employ individuals with differing abilities, proving that inclusion and success can go together. What started as a small idea has blossomed into a global brand with a powerful social mission.

In summary, people/planet impacts can be a compelling reason to start a business. While there are challenges, the potential benefits, including making a difference, gaining community support, and personal fulfillment, make it a worthwhile pursuit.

Lifestyle Choice

In small business terms, a lifestyle choice is the deliberate decision to start a business that aligns with one's values, goals, and desired way of living. This often prioritizes work-life balance over aggressive growth or high profits.

Work-life balance entails managing work responsibilities and personal life in a way that they support rather than conflict with each other. On one end of the spectrum, a small business owner might work part-time to focus on family and hobbies, while on the other end, someone might work full-time but with flexible hours and location.

Starting a business as a lifestyle choice can be driven by both business and emotional motivations. From a business perspective, owning a small business provides control over work hours, workload, and work environment. Emotionally, it offers the satisfaction of aligning work with personal passions and life goals, leading to a more fulfilling career.

There are several advantages to starting a business for lifestyle reasons. Achieving a better work-life balance is a significant benefit. This balance allows for more family time, contributing to stronger family bonds and the potential for better-adjusted children.

Flexibility is another advantage, as it enables business owners to set their schedules, work from home, and take breaks as needed. This flexibility can also lead to cost savings, as there might be less need for commuting, daycare, or renting office space.

Moreover, running a business from home can reduce expenses related to professional attire, meals out, and transportation. The flexibility can also extend to attending important family events and taking vacations without needing to request time off from a superior. These factors collectively contribute to a lower stress level and higher overall satisfaction with life.

Unfortunately, there are also notable disadvantages to choosing a business for lifestyle reasons. Limited growth potential is a primary concern, as lifestyle businesses often prioritize personal time over business expansion. This can lead to potential instability, especially if the market or economic conditions change unfavorably.

Running a business with a small team or no team at all can result in monotony and a lack of diverse perspectives, which can stifle innovation and creativity. Additionally, lifestyle businesses might not generate sufficient profit to provide for retirement, posing a long-term financial risk.

In summary, choosing to start a business as a lifestyle choice can offer priceless benefits, including better work-life balance, flexibility, and cost savings. However, it also comes with challenges such as limited growth potential, potential instability, and insufficient profits for long-term financial security. Weighing these pros and cons carefully can help potential entrepreneurs make informed decisions that align with their life goals and financial needs.

Chapter Recap

This chapter explored several motivations for starting a business, each shaped by personal goals and circumstances.

We began with the desire for independence. This drive allows entrepreneurs to set their schedules, make decisions autonomously, and create a work environment aligned with their values. Next, we discussed financial goals—these range from achieving a livable income to amassing wealth, each with its challenges and rewards.

We then emphasized the importance of passion and interest. While interest might spark the initial idea, passion fuels long-term commitment and success. Market opportunities were also explored, highlighting how identifying and capitalizing on gaps can lead to significant growth. However, it requires thorough market analysis to navigate volatility and competition.

Unforeseen personal circumstances, such as retrenchment or health issues, can also drive individuals to entrepreneurship. These situations present both opportunities and challenges. We also discussed social and environmental impact, emphasizing that businesses can be powerful tools for positive change. They offer dual benefits of profit and contributing to societal and ecological well-being.

Finally, we explored lifestyle choices. Despite some limitations, the desire for a balanced work-life dynamic can be a compelling reason to start a business.

In the next chapter, we will consider key business components. This will provide a comprehensive overview of what it takes to build and sustain a successful business.

Action Plan

Entrepreneurs who are already in business can take a little time to ensure that their reasons for starting the business are aligned with their personal goals. If not, now is an excellent time to clarify this.

For prospective entrepreneurs still contemplating the idea of going into business, I can suggest the following:

1. Carefully consider the reasons we discussed in this chapter.

2. Write down the reason that resonates with you. If there are more than one, jot them down too.

3. Take time to decide whether these reasons are how you truly feel and how you think about your future. Adjust your list - the more clearly you describe this, the better.

4. Once you clearly understand your reason(s) for going into business, you can work on understanding the potential disadvantages. This understanding will positively impact your planning.

For both groups, I suggest you share your thoughts with family and friends, especially that one person who will likely be your most significant pillar of support, your spouse.Also, network with entrepreneurs that are already doing what you intend to do. Learn from other people's experiences and, importantly, learn from success.

Chapter 2
Key Business Components to Consider

"A business absolutely devoted to good service will have only one worry about profits. They will be embarrassingly large" — Henry Ford

Overview

In the previous chapter, we explored several reasons why individuals decide to start their businesses. This understanding of motivations and aspirations sets the stage for our next discussion.

This chapter will guide you through seven key business components. These components are crucial for helping prospective and new entrepreneurs make informed decisions about starting a business or choosing the type of business that aligns with their goals and circumstances. We will not focus on planning or managing these components but on understanding how their unique attributes can affect overall business risk.

First, we will delve into capital, examining how the availability and management of financial resources impact business stability and growth. Next, we will discuss labor, highlighting the challenges associated with human capital. Technology will be our third focus, exploring how it could affect business operations.

Following that, we will cover the profit margin, emphasizing how different profit margins can influence business sustainability. Product attributes will be our fifth component, where we will discuss how the features and quality of your products can affect market acceptance and risk. Market phenomena will be following, providing insights into how market trends and external factors can create risks and opportunities. Finally, we will explore market segmentation, focusing on how identifying and targeting specific customer groups can minimize marketing risks and optimize efforts.

By the end of this chapter, you will have a solid understanding of these seven components and how they interconnect, helping you to make well-informed decisions about the type of business you want to start.

Capital

Capital is the lifeblood of any business. It is the financial resources needed to start, operate, and grow a business. Without sufficient capital, even the most brilliant business idea cannot come to fruition. Capital ensures that a business can buy the necessary assets, pay its expenses, and invest in opportunities for growth and expansion.

There are essentially two primary sources of capital: equity and debt. Equity capital is money invested in the business by its owners or shareholders. This type of capital does not need to be repaid, but it does involve giving up a part of ownership and, potentially, control of the business.

On the other hand, debt capital is money borrowed from external sources, such as banks or other financial institutions. Debt must be repaid with interest, and it does not dilute ownership. However, it requires regular payments, which can strain the business's cash flow.

During the start-up phase, capital is used to cover initial expenses such as buying equipment, securing a location, and funding product development. This stage often requires substantial investment, as the business has not yet generated revenue.

Once the business is operational, capital is needed for day-to-day expenses such as salaries, rent, utilities, and inventory – working capital. Adequate working capital ensures that these operational needs are met without interruption.

As the business grows, more capital is needed for expansion activities, such as opening new locations, launching new products, or entering new markets. Growth capital enables a business to scale and seize new opportunities, further solidifying its market position.

When considering the unique attributes of capital, it is crucial to understand the concept of capital intensity. A capital-intensive business requires a significant amount of financial investment to produce goods or services. Examples of capital-intensive industries include manufacturing, aviation, and telecommunications. These businesses need substantial capital to buy equipment, maintain infrastructure, and cover high operational costs.

Conversely, low-capital-intensity businesses or industries require minimal financial investment to start and operate. Examples include consultancy services, freelance writing, graphic design, and other professional services. These businesses primarily rely on the skills and expertise of the people involved, with lower overhead costs and minimal need for expensive equipment or facilities.

A high capital requirement can be a significant risk for businesses. It means that a large amount of money must be invested before the business can start generating revenue. High capital requirements also increase this risk, as businesses must secure substantial funding and manage large debts or equity investments. If the business does not generate sufficient returns, it can quickly become financially unsustainable.

A high capital requirement acts as a barrier to entry not only for competitors but also for the entrepreneur. It limits the number of individuals who can afford to enter the industry, reducing competition. However, for the entrepreneur, it means that significant financial resources are needed to start the business, which can be a daunting and risky endeavor. The need for substantial capital can lead to reliance on external funding, increasing debt levels, and financial pressure.

One real-life example of a business that failed due to massive capital requirements is Solyndra. Solyndra was a solar panel manufacturer that received over $500 million in government loans and private investment. Despite this substantial capital injection, Solyndra faced high production costs and intense competition from low-cost manufacturers in China. The company struggled to achieve profitability and, ultimately, filed for bankruptcy in 2011. Solyndra's failure highlights how high capital requirements can lead to financial strain and business failure, even with significant investment.

In conclusion, capital is essential for the creation, operation, and growth of a business. High capital intensity can be a barrier to entry and a source of financial risk, making it a critical factor to consider when starting a business.

Labor

Labor, in business terms, refers to the human effort used in the production of goods and services. It encompasses all the work done by employees, from physical tasks to intellectual contributions. Labor is a critical component of any business as it directly influences productivity, quality, and operational efficiency.

Labor-intensive businesses require a large workforce to operate effectively. These businesses depend heavily on human labor rather than machinery or automation. An example of a labor-intensive industry is the hospitality sector, including hotels and resorts. These businesses rely on many employees to provide services, maintain facilities, and ensure customer satisfaction.

On the other end of the spectrum, industries like software development are less labor-intensive. They rely more on technology and automation, requiring fewer employees to produce and maintain their products.

Managing labor can be inherently challenging due to several factors. Recruitment is one of the primary challenges. Finding and hiring suitable candidates is time-consuming and costly. Moreover, the success rate of selecting the right candidates can be low, leading to high turnover rates and added recruitment cycles.

Training is another significant issue, especially in industries that require specialized skills. Training new employees can be expensive and time-consuming. It often takes a considerable amount of time before a new hire becomes fully productive. For instance, in the healthcare industry, training requirements are extensive and costly, affecting the overall efficiency and costs of the business.

Legal complexities add another layer of difficulty to labor management. Hiring and firing employees involves navigating complex legal requirements to ensure compliance with labor laws. These laws vary by region and can be intricate, requiring businesses to invest in legal expertise.

Additionally, payroll management involves adhering to various regulations about wages, taxes, and benefits, further complicating the process.

The risk of losing key personnel or entire teams to competitors poses a significant threat to businesses. When key employees leave, they take valuable knowledge and skills with them. This loss can disrupt operations and negatively affect the business's competitive edge. For example, if a top-performing sales team leaves for a competitor, it can result in a substantial loss of revenue and market share.

A real-life example of a business that failed due to labor issues is the American retailer Circuit City. Circuit City was once a leading electronics retailer in the United States. However, a series of poor management decisions about labor contributed to its downfall.

The company decided to lay off its experienced, higher-paid sales staff and replace them with lower-paid, less experienced workers. This move led to a significant decline in customer service quality. Consequently, customer satisfaction plummeted, and sales dropped. The company was unable to recover from the negative impact of these labor issues and eventually filed for bankruptcy in 2008.

In conclusion, labor is a crucial part of any business but managing it effectively can be fraught with challenges. Recruitment, training, legal requirements, and the risk of losing key personnel are all factors that make labor management complex. Entrepreneurs should be clear about these challenges when contemplating a specific business or industry.

Technology

Technology encompasses the tools, machines, and processes that businesses use to operate efficiently and competitively. It goes far beyond computer hardware and software, touching every industry in diverse ways.

From biotechnology in animal breeding to satellites in communication and robotics in manufacturing, technology drives progress and innovation. Every business, regardless of its size or sector, relies on some form of technology to deliver its products or services.

Staying up to date with relevant technology is crucial for most businesses, except perhaps very small lifestyle businesses. The rapid pace of technological advancement means that falling behind can quickly make a business obsolete.

For example, in the retail sector, advancements in e-commerce, inventory management systems, and customer relationship management (CRM) software have revolutionized business operations. Companies that do not adopt these technologies struggle to compete with more agile and technologically savvy competitors.

A notable example of a business that ignored technological advances and went bankrupt is Blockbuster. Once a dominant player in the video rental industry, Blockbuster did not adapt to the shift toward digital streaming and online rentals.

Despite having the opportunity to buy Netflix in its early days, Blockbuster chose to stick with its traditional brick-and-mortar model. As a result, it couldn't compete with the convenience and affordability of online streaming services. Blockbuster's inability to embrace modern technology ultimately led to its bankruptcy in 2010. This serves as a cautionary tale for businesses about the importance of staying current with technological trends.

Entrepreneurs considering starting a business must identify the technologies at play in their industry. Understanding how these technologies impact operations, marketing, and customer interactions is vital.

Additionally, they should be aware of potential inventions and innovations that could disrupt their industry. For example, in the manufacturing sector, the rise of 3D printing technology has dramatically changed production processes. Companies that recognized and adopted 3D printing early on gained a competitive edge. Conversely, those who ignored it found themselves struggling to keep up.

Being proactive about technology also involves anticipating future trends. This foresight allows businesses to pivot and adapt before they are forced to by market pressures. Entrepreneurs should continually educate themselves about emerging technologies and consider how these could enhance or threaten their business models.

In conclusion, technology is an integral part of every industry and business. Staying up to date with technological advancements is essential for maintaining competitiveness and relevance. Ignoring technology can lead to significant setbacks, as illustrated by Blockbuster's decline.

Entrepreneurs must understand the technologies influencing their industry and remain vigilant about future innovations. By doing so, they can better position their businesses for long-term success.

Profit Margin

Profit margin is the difference between the cost of producing or buying a product and the price at which it is sold. It is the percentage of the sale price – the revenue – that exceeds the costs of the item or goods sold.

A higher profit margin shows that a business keeps more profit for each dollar of sales after covering its costs.

Profit margins can vary widely across different industries. For instance, grocery stores typically operate with low profit margins, often around 2-3%. Some chain convenience stores can reach margins of 20%.

In contrast, specialty or niche retailers can reach a 50% margin, while software companies can enjoy even higher profit margins, sometimes exceeding 70%. These variations are due to differences in business models, cost structures, and market conditions.

Discussing profit margin is crucial when deciding to start a business because it profoundly affects several other components. First, it influences the capital required. Businesses with low profit margins need higher sales volumes to generate the same amount of profit as those with high margins. This often requires more significant investments in inventory, infrastructure, and marketing. For example, a grocery store needs to sell enormous quantities of goods at low margins to cover its costs and generate profit. This demands substantial initial and ongoing capital investment.

Second, profit margin affects decisions around pricing and product mix. A business with a low profit margin must carefully consider its pricing strategy to remain competitive while covering costs. It may need to diversify its product mix to include higher-margin items to boost overall profitability. On the other hand, businesses with high profit margins have more flexibility in pricing and can focus on high-value products without the same pressure to increase sales volume.

Third, profit margin affects breakeven and profitability. A low-margin business must achieve higher sales volumes to reach its breakeven point and become profitable. This can be challenging, especially in competitive markets.

Additionally, low margins limit the ability to offer discounts or promotions without eroding profitability. In contrast, a high-margin business can reach its breakeven point more quickly and has more leeway to offer discounts and incentives to attract customers.

The advantage of a high profit margin is significant. It provides a buffer against market fluctuations, higher operational costs, and competitive pressures.

High-margin businesses can invest more in innovation, marketing, and customer service, creating a competitive edge. They also have more resources to withstand economic downturns and invest in long-term growth strategies.

A real-life example of a business that failed due to a low profit margin is Borders Group, the bookstore chain. Borders struggled with low profit margins in the highly competitive book retail market. The costs associated with running large brick-and-mortar stores and managing extensive inventories outstripped the slim margins from book sales.

Also, Borders did not adapt to the rise of digital books and online sales, which further squeezed its margins. Ultimately, the company's inability to generate sufficient profit led to its bankruptcy in 2011.

In conclusion, profit margin is a critical component to consider when starting a business. It influences capital requirements, pricing strategies, product mix decisions, and the ability to achieve profitability. High profit margins offer significant advantages, including financial stability and flexibility. Conversely, low profit margins can pose substantial challenges, as illustrated by the downfall of Borders Group. Entrepreneurs must carefully evaluate the profit margins in their chosen industry before taking the plunge.

Product Attributes

For the purposes of this book, we will discuss three key categories of product attributes: perishability, handling and storage, and quality and safety. Understanding these aspects is crucial for entrepreneurs to manage risks and ensure the success of their businesses.

Perishable products have limited shelf lives, meaning they deteriorate over time. Shelf life is the duration a product stays usable and safe for consumption. An expiration date is the final day a product is considered safe to use.

For example, fresh produce like strawberries has a noticeably short shelf life, often just a few days. On the other hand, canned goods can last for years without spoiling. Managing perishable products requires careful planning to minimize waste and ensure product quality.

Handling and storage present added challenges and risks. Proper storage conditions are essential to maintaining product quality and safety, and factors such as temperature, humidity, and light exposure must be controlled. For instance, frozen foods require continuous refrigeration to prevent spoilage. This need for constant cold storage can be a significant challenge for businesses, especially during transportation and distribution.

A real-life example of a business that went under due to handling and storage problems is Zaycon Fresh. Zaycon Fresh was a small company that provided fresh meat products directly to consumers at wholesale prices. They faced significant challenges with their cold storage and logistics. Poor handling practices led to spoilage and food safety issues, resulting in a loss of customer trust. The company could not maintain the quality of its products during transportation and storage, leading to its closure in 2018.

On the other hand, a business that became hugely successful due to its innovation in handling and storage is HelloFresh. HelloFresh is a meal kit delivery service that revolutionized the way fresh ingredients are packaged and delivered. By developing innovative packaging solutions that maintain the freshness and quality of ingredients during transit, HelloFresh ensured customer satisfaction. Their efficient handling and storage practices allowed them to expand rapidly and become a leader in the meal kit industry.

Statutory testing and labeling involve adhering to regulatory standards for product safety and information disclosure. This process can be complex and costly, consuming significant resources. Products must undergo various tests to ensure they meet safety standards and are correctly labeled.

For example, pharmaceutical companies must conduct extensive clinical trials and safety tests before bringing a new drug to market. These requirements can delay product launches and add substantial costs.

In conclusion, understanding product attributes is vital for managing business risks. Perishability requires careful inventory management and efficient supply chains. Handling and storage demand proper facilities and logistics to maintain product quality. Statutory testing and labeling add layers of complexity and cost but are necessary for ensuring safety and compliance.

Prospective entrepreneurs should be aware of these challenges and prepare accordingly to navigate them successfully.

Market Phenomena

Market phenomena refer to the various patterns and behaviors seen in markets that can significantly impact businesses.

These phenomena include fads, trends, cycles, and seasonal variations. Understanding these aspects is essential for entrepreneurs as they decide on the type of business to venture into.

A fad is a temporary, highly popular product or service that experiences a rapid rise and fall in consumer interest. An example of a fad is the fidget spinner, which gained immense popularity in 2017. Fads offer the advantage of quick profits due to high demand in a short period of time. However, they also come with the risk of sudden obsolescence. Investing heavily in a fad can lead to significant losses if the market moves on quickly.

A trend is a longer-lasting change in consumer behavior or preferences. Unlike fads, trends develop over time and have a more sustained impact. An example of a trend is the increasing demand for organic food.

Trends provide businesses with more stability and potential for growth. They allow for better long-term planning and investment. However, trends also require businesses to adapt continuously and stay updated with market changes to remain competitive.

When it comes to cycles, we will look at business cycles and product life cycles.

Business cycles refer to regular patterns of expansion and contraction in economic activity. They affect businesses by influencing consumer spending, investment, and overall economic health. During economic expansions, businesses often experience growth and increased sales. Conversely, during recessions, businesses may face reduced demand and financial challenges. Understanding business cycles helps entrepreneurs plan for economic fluctuations.

Product life cycles describe the stages a product goes through, from introduction to decline. These stages include introduction, growth, maturity, and then decline. Each stage presents different challenges and opportunities for businesses.

In the introduction stage, businesses focus on marketing and building awareness. During the growth stage, sales increase rapidly, and competition may intensify. The maturity stage sees sales peak, and businesses must innovate to keep market share. Finally, the decline stage involves a reduction in sales and potential product discontinuation.

A real-life example of a business that became successful with a product but later failed due to the product life cycle is BlackBerry. BlackBerry smartphones were highly popular in the early 2000s, especially among business professionals. However, the company did not innovate and adapt to the shift towards touchscreens and app-driven smartphones. As a result, BlackBerry lost its market share and eventually exited the smartphone market.

Seasonal fluctuations refer to changes in consumer demand that occur at specific times of the year. These variations can significantly affect businesses, particularly those in industries with seasonal peaks and troughs.

An example of a core business sector influenced by seasonal fluctuations is the retail industry, which sees a significant boost in sales during the holiday season. Another example is the tourism industry, where demand peaks during vacation periods and drops during off-seasons, in some cases to almost nothing.

The impact of seasonal demand must be emphasized. In a broader retail context, holiday seasons account for a substantial proportion of annual sales, especially around Christmas, where US consumers spent over $950 billion in 2023. Mother's Day alone has generated upwards of $23 billion annually in the US[1] , showing the significant impact of seasonal shopping.

Businesses affected by seasonal fluctuations must plan their inventory, staffing, and marketing strategies to align with these patterns.

In conclusion, understanding market phenomena is crucial for entrepreneurs when deciding on the type of business to start. Fads, trends, cycles, and seasonal variations each present unique challenges and opportunities.

---

1. Source: National Retail Federation (NRF)

Market Segmentation

Market segmentation is the process of dividing a broad consumer or business market into sub-groups based on shared characteristics. For our purposes, these segments are based on demographics, geographic areas, psychographics, and behavior.

Market segmentation allows businesses to target specific groups more effectively. They can tailor their marketing efforts and meet the unique needs of each segment. By understanding and catering to these specific segments, businesses can improve customer satisfaction, loyalty, and profitability.

Including market segmentation in this chapter is essential because some segments require special attention due to their inherent risks. Entrepreneurs must be aware of these risks and prepare to manage them accordingly.

Market Segmentation Based on Demographics

Low-income demographics: These segments often have limited financial resources, increasing the risk of payment defaults or product returns. For example, businesses targeting low-income consumers must carefully consider pricing strategies. They should offer affordable payment plans to mitigate these risks.

Youth and elderly: These groups might have specific needs or vulnerabilities that increase risk. For instance, products targeting young children must adhere to strict safety standards. Services for the elderly may need to address mobility and accessibility concerns.

Market Segmentation Based on Geographics

Emerging markets: While offering significant growth opportunities, these markets can also pose higher risks due to economic instability, political uncertainties, and infrastructure challenges. Businesses entering emerging markets must conduct thorough research and develop strategies to navigate these potential pitfalls.

Disaster-prone regions: Areas susceptible to natural disasters carry inherent risks for businesses operating there. Companies must invest in robust risk management plans, including insurance and contingency strategies, to protect their operations and assets.

Market Segmentation Based on Psychographics

Impulsive buyers: Customers with a tendency to make spontaneous purchases might lead to higher return rates or payment defaults. Businesses targeting this segment need to implement clear return policies and watch payment behaviors closely.

Price-sensitive customers: While attractive to businesses, this segment might be more likely to switch to competitors based on price fluctuations. Companies must balance competitive pricing with maintaining profitability and customer loyalty.

Market Segmentation Based on Behavior

New customers: These customers have a higher risk of churning or failing to meet expectations. Businesses should focus on onboarding strategies and customer support to improve retention rates and satisfaction.

High-value customers: While desirable, these customers often require more attention and resources, potentially increasing costs. Companies must ensure they can provide the necessary level of service and support to support these valuable relationships without overextending their resources.

In conclusion, market segmentation is a powerful tool for businesses to target and serve diverse customer groups effectively. However, some segments present unique challenges and risks that entrepreneurs must be prepared to manage. By understanding the specific needs and behaviors of different market segments, businesses can develop strategies to mitigate risks and capitalize on opportunities.

Chapter Recap

In this chapter, we explored several key business components crucial for entrepreneurs to consider. These components can significantly influence the type of business you decide to start and how you manage it.

First, we discussed capital. Capital is the lifeblood of any business, and understanding its sources and uses is essential. We examined the differences between equity and debt capital and the implications of capital intensity on business operations.

Next, we covered labor. Labor encompasses the human effort in a business, from recruitment to training and retention. We highlighted the challenges associated with managing labor, such as the costs and complexities of hiring and the risk of losing key personnel.

Technology was another vital component. It affects all industries, and staying current with technological advancements is crucial for business success. We provided examples of businesses that failed because they ignored technological changes and those that thrived because of innovation.

Profit margin was also discussed. We defined it and explained its importance in business decision-making. We examined how profit margin affects pricing, capital requirements, and overall profitability. Additionally, we gave an example of a business that failed due to a low profit margin.

We then explored product attributes. We focused on perishability, handling and storage, and quality and safety. Each attribute poses unique challenges that require careful management. We provided real-life examples to illustrate these points.

Market phenomena were also covered. We looked at fads, trends, cycles, and seasonal variations. Understanding these phenomena helps businesses adapt and thrive in changing market conditions.

Finally, we discussed market segmentation. Segmenting the market allows businesses to target specific groups more effectively. We examined various segments based on demographics, geographic areas, psychographics, and behavior. Each segment presents unique opportunities and risks.

In the next chapter, we will explore ways to categorize businesses and the various types of businesses.

Action Plan

Both existing and prospective entrepreneurs will benefit from spending time sharpening their understanding of the components most relevant to their business or likely to influence them in the future.

Existing entrepreneurs

1. List all the components that are relevant to your business, including the specific risks.

2. Make a list of specific aspects you need to research or learn to mitigate those risks.

3. Start crafting an implementation plan, and don't wait until you have all the answers; implement as and when you find a solution. Small, immediate gains can be a game changer.

Prospective entrepreneurs

1. List those business components you want to avoid altogether.

2. Separately, list those components that you are comfortable with, have knowledge about, and that you can manage.

3. Measure all business opportunities against these two lists to find a business that fits your preferences and your goals.

Chapter 3
Types of Businesses – Legal Structure

"The secret of getting ahead is getting started. The secret of getting started is breaking your complex overwhelming tasks into small manageable tasks, and then starting on the first one" — *Mark Twain*

In the previous chapters, we explored the reasons why one would choose to embark on this journey and key business components to consider. Now, it's time to discuss the diverse types of businesses you can start, laying the groundwork for understanding the broad landscape of entrepreneurship.

Overview

When considering the various types of businesses, it becomes clear that there are multiple ways to categorize or describe them. This chapter will focus on the first of two primary classifications, namely the legal structure. There are several distinct types, each with its advantages and challenges.

The chapter will cover sole proprietorships, partnerships, limited liability companies, and corporations. Understanding the legal implications of each structure is crucial, as it impacts everything from tax obligations to personal liability.

Throughout the chapter, we will provide a balanced view of the pros and cons of each type. By the end, you should clearly understand which legal structure aligns best with your goals, along with insights into any further details you may need to pursue your vision effectively.

Sole Proprietorship

A sole proprietorship is the simplest and most common form of business. It is an unincorporated business owned and operated by one individual, with no distinction between the business and the owner. This means the owner receives all profits and is responsible for all the business's debts, losses, and liabilities. This structure is popular due to its ease of setup and minimal regulatory paperwork. No complex legal requirements make it an attractive option for many new entrepreneurs.

In the UK and Canada, the concept of a sole proprietorship is similar to that in the US, with the business and the owner being legally indistinguishable. In both countries, sole proprietors are personally responsible for all profits, debts, and liabilities.

However, while the basic structure is the same, there are differences in tax obligations and regulatory paperwork. For example, in the UK, sole traders must register with HM Revenue & Customs (HMRC). In Canada, sole proprietors must report their business income on their personal tax returns and may need to register for a GST/HST number, depending on revenue. Despite these differences, both countries maintain the simplicity and ease of setting up a sole proprietorship.

Pros of a Sole Proprietor

One of the main advantages of a sole proprietorship is complete control. The owner makes all the decisions and has the final say in all matters. This autonomy allows for swift decision-making and the ability to pivot the business direction quickly. The setup process is also straightforward and inexpensive, often requiring just a business license or a business name filing. There are fewer formalities and lower startup costs compared to other business structures. This simplicity allows the owner to focus more on running the business than dealing with administrative burdens. The direct connection to business operations also means the owner can build personal relationships with customers and suppliers, which can be a significant advantage in service-oriented businesses.

Cons of a Sole Proprietor

However, the simplicity of a sole proprietorship comes with significant downsides. The owner has unlimited personal liability, meaning personal assets can be at risk if the business incurs debt or faces legal issues. This can be a substantial risk, especially in industries prone to lawsuits or high debt levels. Additionally, it can be harder to raise capital, as investors are less likely to invest in unincorporated businesses. Banks and other financial institutions may view sole proprietorships as higher risk, leading to challenges in securing loans or lines of credit. Entrepreneurs often need help keeping business and personal finances separate, which can complicate accounting and tax filings. Personal liability can also affect the owner's credit score and financial stability if the business faces financial difficulties. Moreover, sole proprietorships might lack the perceived credibility of more structured business forms, impacting relationships with larger clients or suppliers.

Despite these challenges, it's important to note that a sole proprietorship can be converted to another structure as the business grows and evolves. This flexibility allows owners to start and expand as needed. The ability to transition to a partnership or company offers a pathway for growth and additional legal protection as the business's needs become more complex. This adaptability makes the sole proprietorship a viable starting point for many entrepreneurs, who can scale and re-structure their business as it matures.

Partnership

A partnership is an organization where two or more individuals share ownership. Each partner contributes to the business and shares in its profits and losses. Different forms of partnerships include general partnerships, limited partnerships (LP), and limited liability partnerships (LLP). In a general partnership, all partners share equal responsibility for managing the business. They also assume liability for business debts and obligations. Limited partnerships consist of at least one general partner who manages the business and one or more limited partners who invest in the business but do not participate in day-to-day operations. Limited liability partnerships offer protection from personal liability for business debts. They are often used by professional groups such as law and accounting firms.

In both the UK and Canada, partnerships are similar to the US model, with some distinctions.

In the UK, partnerships operate under the Partnership Act 1890. Like the US, general partnerships involve shared management and liability among partners. The UK also has limited partnerships (LP) and limited liability partnerships (LLP), with LLPs offering personal liability protection.

In Canada, partnerships are governed by provincial laws. While the structure of general partnerships, limited partnerships, and LLPs is similar, LLPs are only available to certain professions, such as lawyers and accountants, much like in the US.

In both countries, the liability protections and registration requirements may vary slightly by jurisdiction but align closely with U.S. practices.

Pros of a Partnership

The primary advantage of a partnership is shared responsibility. Partners can combine their resources, skills, and expertise to run the business. This collaboration often leads to better decision-making and problem-solving. Each partner brings unique strengths and perspectives, which can enhance the business's overall performance. Partnerships also benefit from pass-through taxation. This means profits are taxed only once at the individual level. Moreover, partnerships can pool financial resources, making raising capital easier than a sole proprietorship. Multiple partners' combined resources and efforts can increase business opportunities and growth potential.

Cons of a Partnership

Despite these benefits, partnerships have notable downsides. Shared liability means that each partner is personally liable for the business's debts and obligations. This can lead to potential conflicts, especially if partners have different visions or work ethics. Misunderstandings and disagreements can strain the partnership and affect the business's operations.

As a financier, I am wary of partnerships, particularly informal ones. Often, I ask partners if they know the difference between a partnership and a sinking ship. This question sometimes jolts them into formalizing the partnership prudently, with clear agreements and legal structures in place.

Partnerships in professional practices, such as law or accounting firms, are typically more formal and structured. However, all partnerships must have a well-defined partnership agreement to mitigate risks and manage expectations. This agreement should outline each partner's roles, responsibilities, and how conflicts will be resolved. Without an explicit agreement, partnerships can quickly become unmanageable, leading to legal disputes and the dissolution of the business.

In summary, partnerships offer advantages in terms of shared responsibility and resources. However, they also come with significant risks and challenges. Proper planning, clear agreements, and legal structures are essential to managing these risks and ensuring a successful partnership. By addressing potential conflicts and liabilities upfront, partners can create a solid foundation for their business and work together towards common goals.

Limited Liability Company (LLC)

A Limited Liability Company (LLC) is a hybrid business structure that combines the benefits of a corporation and a partnership. It provides its owners, known as members, with limited liability protection, meaning they are not personally liable for the company's debts or liabilities. An LLC can have one or many members and is recognized as a separate legal entity from its owners. This structure is popular because it offers flexibility in management and fewer regulatory requirements than corporations.

In the UK, there is no direct equivalent to the US LLC. Instead, the closest counterpart is the Limited Company (Ltd), which similarly provides limited liability protection to its owners (called shareholders) and is recognized as a separate legal entity. Unlike an LLC, a Limited Company must adhere to stricter regulatory requirements, such as filing annual financial statements and holding annual meetings.

In Canada, the equivalent structure is a Corporation rather than an LLC. Canadian corporations provide limited liability protection to their shareholders, but unlike an LLC, a corporation is subject to more stringent regulations and may face double taxation unless designated as a small business corporation (SBC), which allows for special tax considerations.

Pros of an LLC

One of the main advantages of an LLC is limited liability. Members are protected from personal liability for business debts and claims. Personal assets like a home or car are usually safe from creditors. Additionally, an LLC offers flexible management options. Members can manage the business themselves or hire managers to oversee the operations. This flexibility allows for various management structures, which can be tailored to the needs of the business. LLCs also benefit from pass-through taxation, where business income is reported on the members' tax returns, avoiding the double taxation corporations face.

In the UK, a Limited Company (Ltd) also offers limited liability, protecting the owners' personal assets from business liabilities, much like an LLC in the US. Additionally, a Limited Company offers flexible management options but with more formal requirements, such as the need for company directors and shareholders meetings.

In Canada, corporations provide similar limited liability protection. However, unlike US LLCs, Canadian corporations do not benefit from pass-through taxation. Instead, they are taxed at the corporate level, and dividends distributed to shareholders are taxed again as personal income, though small business corporations may enjoy reduced tax rates.

Cons of an LLC

Despite these benefits, there are some drawbacks to forming an LLC. One significant disadvantage is the cost. Setting up an LLC involves one-time fees, such as filing the articles of organization. There are also recurring annual fees and compliance costs. These costs can add up, especially for small businesses. Another challenge is the complexity of the setup. While not as complicated as forming a corporation, creating an LLC still requires careful planning and documentation. Owners must draft an operating agreement outlining the business's management structure and operating procedures. This agreement helps prevent misunderstandings among members and provides a clear plan for the business's operation.

Setting up a Limited Company in the UK also involves costs, such as registration fees with Companies House and ongoing compliance costs for filing annual accounts and reports. However, the regulatory burden for a Limited Company is typically heavier than for a US LLC.

In Canada, forming a corporation involves higher upfront and ongoing fees as well, like an LLC in the US. Additionally, Canadian corporations require more formal documentation, such as articles of incorporation, bylaws, and annual shareholder meetings, which can add to the complexity and administrative burden compared to US LLCs.

In summary, an LLC offers the benefits of limited liability and flexible management, making it an attractive option for business owners. However, the costs and complexity of establishing and maintaining an LLC should be carefully considered. Despite these challenges, many find that the advantages of an LLC outweigh the drawbacks, making it a popular choice for businesses of all sizes.

The LLC would be my preferred option of the three legal structures we have discussed thus far. The perceived difficulty of setting it up can easily be overcome through research and further reading.

Corporation

A corporation is a business structure that runs as a separate legal entity from its owners. It is owned by shareholders who invest capital in exchange for ownership shares. The corporation is liable for business debts and obligations, protecting shareholders' personal assets. This structure is often used by businesses that require substantial capital and have many employees. Corporations can range from small businesses to multinational enterprises with thousands of employees and significant financial resources.

In the UK, corporations are known as Limited Companies (Ltd) or Public Limited Companies (PLC). These companies are also separate legal entities from their owners, with shareholders holding ownership through shares. Similar to the US, shareholders' personal assets are protected from business liabilities. However, a Public Limited Company (PLC) is required to have a higher minimum share capital and must offer shares to the public, making it more aligned with larger corporations.

In Canada, corporations function in much the same way as in the US, with shareholders owning the company and enjoying protection from liability. Both private and public corporations exist, and the legal entity is separate from its owners. Like in the US, Canadian corporations are subject to stringent regulatory requirements and can be small private companies or large public corporations.

Pros of a Corporation

One of the primary advantages of a corporation is limited liability. Shareholders are not personally liable for the corporation's debts or legal obligations that protect their assets. Another significant benefit is the ability to raise capital easily. Corporations can issue stocks and bonds to attract investors, providing the necessary funds for expansion and operations.

This ability to raise large amounts of capital makes corporations well-suited for businesses needing substantial investment. Additionally, corporations have perpetual existence, meaning they continue to exist even if ownership or management changes. This stability can attract investors and help in long-term business planning.

In both the UK and Canada, limited liability and the ability to raise capital through share issuing are key advantages for corporations, like the US.

In the UK, Public Limited Companies (PLC) can raise capital from the public by issuing shares on the stock market, making them attractive for businesses with high capital needs. However, this comes with higher regulatory standards than private companies. Limited Companies (Ltd), on the other hand, cannot offer shares to the public but still provide limited liability and protection for shareholders.

In Canada, corporations have a similar advantage when it comes to raising capital by issuing shares or bonds. Canadian corporations also enjoy perpetual existence, which allows them to continue operations through ownership changes, just like US corporations. Tax incentives for small businesses in Canada (like the Small Business Deduction) can also make corporations attractive for growth and long-term planning.

Cons of a Corporation

Despite these advantages, corporations have significant drawbacks. One major disadvantage is double taxation. The corporation pays taxes on its profits at the corporate level. Then, shareholders pay taxes again on any dividends they receive. This double taxation can reduce the overall profitability of the business.

Furthermore, corporations face overly complex regulatory requirements. They must adhere to stringent reporting and compliance standards, which can be time-consuming and costly. This includes keeping detailed financial records, holding regular board meetings, and filing annual reports. The high setup costs are another disadvantage.

Forming a corporation involves substantial legal and administrative expenses, including filing fees, legal fees, and ongoing compliance costs. These costs can be prohibitive for small businesses or startups with limited financial resources.

In the UK, corporations (especially PLCs) also face double taxation, as profits are taxed at the corporate level and dividends are taxed again when distributed to shareholders, just like in the US. Private Limited Companies (Ltd) face similar challenges, although the tax regime in the UK can offer some relief through allowances and deductions. In Canada, double taxation similarly applies, although shareholders can receive a dividend tax credit to offset part of the taxation on dividends.

Both UK and Canadian corporations must also comply with complex regulatory requirements, including filing annual accounts, holding board meetings, and adhering to governance standards, which can be costly and time-consuming. As in the US, the high costs of forming and maintaining a corporation in the UK and Canada can be prohibitive for small businesses or startups. In Canada, the cost of incorporating varies by province, adding another layer of complexity.

In summary, corporations offer significant benefits such as limited liability and the ability to raise substantial amounts of capital. However, they also come with considerable challenges, including double taxation, complex regulatory requirements, and high setup costs.

A corporation will not be the preferred legal structure for this book and the series.

Chapter Recap

In this chapter, we explored different types of businesses based on legal structure, including the pros and cons of each.

In the next chapter, we will look at the next primary classification, namely core business sector.

Action Plan

If you have not yet decided on a legal structure for your business, or you want to make changes, I can suggest the following plan:

1. Decide which legal structure best suits your plans.

2. Make a list of specific questions you have about the structure.

3. Make a list of sources (for example, books, websites, or a business coach) available that can provide the required information.

Chapter 4
Types of Businesses – Core Business Sector

"I don't know the word 'quit.' Either I never did, or I have abolished it" – Susan Butcher

In the first two chapters we explored the reasons why one would choose to embark on this journey, and key business components to consider. Now, it's time to discuss the second primary business classification, namely the core business sector. It will further lay the groundwork for understanding the broad landscape of entrepreneurship.

Overview

Whereas the earlier chapter discussed types of businesses according to legal structures, this chapter discusses them according to their core business sector, also referred to as their primary business type. Understanding different core business sectors is crucial for aspiring entrepreneurs because the industry you choose will influence your business's strategy, operations, and revenue streams.

Core business sectors define the broad categories of businesses based on their primary activities, such as manufacturing, retail, e-commerce, and more. By exploring various core business sectors, you can better find the one that aligns with your business goals and market needs.

In this section, we'll examine the main core business sectors, providing examples and insights into their advantages and disadvantages. Whether you're planning to start a traditional brick-and-mortar store or a tech startup, understanding these sectors will help you make informed decisions and craft a business strategy.

Retail

Retail businesses sell goods or services directly to consumers for their personal use. They use physical stores, online platforms, and mobile apps. Retailers function as intermediaries between manufacturers and consumers, offering products in small quantities to meet individual needs.

In developed countries, the retail sector is a sizable part of the economy. According to the National Retail Federation (NRF)[1] , retail contributes about 20% to the GDP of developed economies. This sector includes a vast array of businesses, from grocery stores and clothing boutiques to online marketplaces and specialty shops.

Characteristics of Retail Businesses

Retail businesses share several key traits that define their operations and market approach. These include:

---

1. The National Retail Federation (NRF) is a U.S.-based organization but operates with a global reach. While its headquarters are in the United States, it is recognized as the world's largest retail trade association, representing retailers and industry stakeholders internationally.

Customer focus is a primary goal, providing a positive experience through personalized service, easy product access, and responsive support.

Product variety is essential, with retailers offering a wide range of products to cater to diverse consumer preferences, often stocking many brands and categories within a single store.

Location and accessibility are strategic, with physical stores located in high-traffic areas such as malls, shopping centers, and urban streets to attract customers.

Sales channels are diverse, including brick-and-mortar stores, e-commerce websites, and mobile apps, to reach a broad customer base.

Inventory management is crucial to ensure product availability while minimizing excess stock and associated costs.

Unconventional Retail Examples

Some retail businesses are not at once recognized as such, surprising many with their retail nature. For instance:

Vending machines are automated retail outlets selling everything from snacks and drinks to electronics and beauty products, offering convenience in high-traffic spots like airports and office buildings.

Farmers' markets, often seen as community events, are retail operations where vendors sell fresh produce, handmade goods, and artisanal products directly to consumers.

Pop-up shops are temporary retail spaces that appear in various locations for short periods. Brands use them to test new markets, launch products, or create unique customer experiences.

Pros of Retail Businesses

Retail businesses offer several advantages that make them appealing to entrepreneurs:

Direct customer interaction allows retailers to engage with customers directly, building relationships and gaining valuable insights into consumer preferences and behaviors.

Tangible product display in physical stores lets customers see, touch, and try products before buying, enhancing the shopping experience and reducing the likelihood of returns.

Brand presence can be enhanced by a well-designed retail space, which attracts more customers and establishes a strong market presence.

Impulse buying is encouraged by retail environments through attractive displays, promotions, and strategic product placements.

Cons of Retail Businesses

Despite the benefits, retail businesses also face many challenges:

High overhead costs in running a retail business, including rent, utilities, salaries, and inventory costs. These overheads can be exceptionally high for physical stores in prime locations.

Inventory management is crucial but challenging, requiring accurate forecasting, efficient stock control, and timely replenishment to avoid stockouts or overstock situations. Slick systems are necessary to achieve that.

The competitive market in the retail sector is intense, with businesses vying for the same customer base. Staying ahead requires constant innovation, marketing efforts, and adapting to changing consumer trends.

Economic sensitivity is a factor, as retail businesses are generally sensitive to economic fluctuations. Consumer spending habits are influenced by factors such as employment rates, inflation, and disposable income.

Retail businesses play a vital role in the economy, providing consumers with access to a wide range of products and services. Understanding the unique characteristics, advantages, and challenges of the retail sector can help entrepreneurs make informed decisions about a possible career as a retail entrepreneur.

Service

The service industry encompasses businesses that provide intangible products or experiences to consumers rather than physical goods. Services can include a wide range of activities, from professional consultations and maintenance work to entertainment and hospitality. Unlike products, services are consumed at the point of delivery and often require a direct interaction between the service provider and the customer.

In developed countries, the service industry is a significant part of the economy. According to the International Monetary Fund (IMF), the service sector is approximately 70% of the GDP in developed economies on average. This dominance reflects the growing demand for a variety of services that enhance the quality of life and support other sectors of the economy.

Characteristics of Service Businesses

Service businesses share distinct characteristics that differentiate them from product-based businesses. These include:

Customer focus is paramount, with service providers prioritizing customer satisfaction and experience. The intangibility of services means that they cannot be seen, touched, or owned, making the quality of the service and the customer experience crucial.

Customization is often crucial, as services can be tailored to meet individual client needs. The delivery process is integral, with the service often produced and consumed simultaneously, requiring the presence and active participation of the customer.

Relationship building is a core aspect, as ongoing interaction and trust between the provider and the customer are essential for repeat business and referrals.

Unconventional Service Examples

Some services are not immediately recognized for what they are, surprising many with their unique nature. For instance:

Pet therapy services provide trained animals to visit hospitals, nursing homes, and schools, offering therapeutic benefits through interaction with patients and students. Virtual interior design services offer online consultations and design plans for home renovations, giving professional advice without the need for in-person visits.

Personal shopping and styling services go beyond traditional retail help, with experts curating personalized wardrobes and shopping experiences for clients. In the service industry, McDonald's is the most recognized brand name globally. While primarily known for its fast food, McDonald's excels in service delivery, emphasizing customer satisfaction, consistency, and operational efficiency.

Pros of Service Businesses

Service businesses offer unique advantages that make them appealing to entrepreneurs:

Lower startup costs are a significant benefit, as many service businesses require minimal investment in physical inventory or manufacturing facilities.

Flexibility is inherent in this sector, allowing providers to adapt their offerings based on customer feedback and market demand.

Direct interaction with customers provides immediate feedback, enabling continuous improvement and strong relationships.

Customization of services allows providers to cater to specific client needs, creating unique value propositions and competitive advantages.

Cons of Service Businesses

Despite the benefits, service businesses also face challenges:

The intangibility of services can make it difficult to demonstrate value to potential customers before they experience the service. Dependence on skills and expertise means that the quality of the service is closely tied to the provider's abilities, requiring ongoing training and professional development.

Low barriers to entry into some industries within this core business sector can lead to high competition, with many new entrants quickly joining the market and driving down prices. Customer expectations and satisfaction are highly variable, requiring constant attention and effort to maintain high service standards.

Service businesses play a vital role in the economy, providing essential and diverse offerings that enhance consumer well-being and support other industries. Given its sizeable contribution to the economy, it is small wonder that many entrepreneurs prefer the service industry as an entrepreneurial start or career.

Manufacturing

Manufacturing is the process of converting raw materials into finished products using machinery, tools, and labor. It plays a crucial role in the economy, providing goods that meet consumer and industrial needs. For this book and the series, we will exclude agriculture and mining from our definition of manufacturing.

Interestingly, manufacturing is often considered the oldest economic activity in the world. After all, humans have been making tools and artifacts since the Stone Age. One example is the creation of stone tools around 2.6 million years ago, according to the Smithsonian Institution. This ancient practice of crafting tools laid the foundation for modern manufacturing.

In developed countries, manufacturing is a significant part of the economy, although it doesn't dominate as it once did. According to the World Bank, manufacturing contributes about 15% to the GDP of developed economies. This sector's importance remains due to its role in producing goods that fuel other economic activities and support various industries.

Characteristics of Manufacturing Businesses

Manufacturing businesses exhibit several defining traits:

The production process involves converting raw materials into finished goods, which can be anything from cars to electronics.

Large-scale operations are typical, with manufacturing facilities often employing hundreds or even thousands of workers to maintain production levels.

Machinery and technology play a central role, as advanced equipment and automated systems enhance efficiency and output.

Quality control is crucial, with stringent measures in place to ensure that products meet specific standards and regulations before reaching the market.

Supply chain management is essential, as manufacturers rely on a steady flow of raw materials and components to maintain continuous production.

Unconventional Manufacturing Examples

Some manufacturers produce items that might surprise you. For instance:

Did you know that perfume manufacturing is a complex process involving the extraction and blending of various natural and synthetic ingredients to create unique scents?

Another surprising example is the production of high-end prosthetics, where advanced materials and precision engineering come together to create life-changing devices for individuals with limb loss.

In the realm of manufacturing, the world's most recognized brand is arguably Apple. Known for its innovative electronics, Apple exemplifies the blend of high technology and manufacturing excellence.

Pros of Manufacturing Businesses

Manufacturing businesses offer several significant advantages:

High barriers to entry exist due to the substantial capital investment required for equipment, facilities, and technology, which reduces competition.

Control over production processes allows manufacturers to maintain high quality and implement efficient practices.

The potential for high profit margins is notable, especially when manufacturing high-demand or specialized products.

The economic impact is considerable, as manufacturing businesses create numerous jobs and contribute to a region's industrial growth.

Cons of Manufacturing Businesses

However, there are also notable challenges:

High capital investment is needed to establish and maintain manufacturing operations, which can be a significant financial burden.

Complex operations require skilled management and a workforce proficient in handling sophisticated machinery and technology.

Regulatory compliance can be demanding, with manufacturers needing to adhere to numerous industry standards and safety regulations.

Environmental impact is another concern, as manufacturing processes can produce waste and emissions that need to be managed responsibly.

Manufacturing businesses remain a cornerstone of the global economy, producing essential goods and driving technological advancements. By understanding the unique characteristics, advantages, and challenges of the manufacturing sector, entrepreneurs can make informed decisions about entering this field.

E-commerce

E-commerce, or electronic commerce, involves buying and selling goods and services over the internet. The very first e-commerce transaction happened on August 11, 1994, when a man sold a Sting CD to his friend through the website NetMarket, making it the first online sale. ZDNet notes this pioneering moment[2].

While e-commerce is a sub-set of retail, its rapid growth and unique characteristics make it worth special mention. Over the past 20 years, e-commerce has revolutionized the way consumers shop and businesses work. According to Statista, e-commerce accounted for about 14.3% of total retail sales in developed countries in 2021. This figure reflects the substantial impact and growth of online shopping in the global economy.

Characteristics of E-commerce Businesses

E-commerce businesses differ from traditional retailers in several ways:

---

2. ZDNet is a technology-focused website that provides news, analysis, and reviews of the latest trends, products, and developments in the tech industry

They operate primarily online, using websites, apps, and digital platforms to reach customers. This eliminates the need for physical storefronts and allows for a broader audience.

The business models in e-commerce vary significantly. Drop-shipping is a standard model where the retailer does not keep goods in stock but transfers customer orders to the manufacturer or wholesaler, who then ships the goods directly to the customer. Another model involves businesses keeping their own warehouses, enabling them to control inventory and shipping processes more closely.

Payment and transaction processes are digital, involving online payment gateways, credit card processing, and digital wallets, which facilitate seamless and secure transactions.

Marketing strategies in e-commerce heavily rely on digital marketing, including SEO, social media advertising, email campaigns, and influencer partnerships to drive traffic and sales.

Unconventional E-commerce Ventures

Some e-commerce ventures are surprising in their uniqueness.

Subscription box services, such as those offering monthly deliveries of niche products like gourmet snacks, craft supplies, or mystery books, have become incredibly popular.

Another unexpected example is the online sale of virtual real estate in the digital world.

In the e-commerce realm, the world's most recognized brand is undoubtedly Amazon. Founded in 1994 by Jeff Bezos, Amazon started as an online bookstore and has since expanded into virtually every retail category. As of 2022, Amazon's estimated annual sales were over $469 billion, highlighting its monumental growth and influence.

Pros of E-commerce Businesses

E-commerce businesses offer many advantages:

Global reach allows businesses to access customers worldwide, breaking down geographical barriers and expanding market potential.

Lower start-up costs are a significant benefit, as online stores do not require the same level of investment in physical infrastructure and can run with leaner staff.

Convenience for customers is a major draw, with 24/7 availability, home delivery options, and easy access to a vast array of products.

Data analytics in e-commerce provides valuable insights into customer behavior, preferences, and trends, enabling businesses to tailor their offerings and marketing strategies more effectively.

Cons of E-commerce Businesses

But, as always, there are challenges to be considered:

High competition in the e-commerce space can make it difficult for new entrants to gain visibility and attract customers.

Technical challenges are inherent in running an online business, including website maintenance, cybersecurity threats, and the need for a robust IT infrastructure.

Logistics and fulfillment can be complex, particularly for businesses that ship products internationally, requiring efficient supply chain management and reliable shipping solutions.

Trust and credibility must be established, as customers can only physically inspect products after buying, which can lead to hesitation and the need for solid customer service and return policies.

E-commerce continues to reshape the retail landscape and is a popular choice for entrepreneurs with a flair for technology. By leveraging its unique characteristics and understanding the market dynamics, prospective, tech-savvy entrepreneurs can find remarkable success in this ever-evolving sector.

Chapter Recap

In this chapter, we explored different types of businesses based on their core business sector. It provided a broad understanding of these diverse business types, aiding aspiring entrepreneurs in deciding which business model best aligns with their goals and values.

In the next chapter, we will look at a third group of businesses, those with unique characteristics.

Action Plan

If you already know what type of business you want to start or already are in business, congratulations! If undecided, there are many sources available to get your mind racing:

1. Self-evaluation. Reflect on what you are passionate about and what you want to achieve. Consider how each business model aligns with your personal and professional aspirations. Make a list of your strong points, areas of expertise, preferences, interests, and passions. On

the negative side, make a list of things, situations, and environments that you are not interested in. Periodically review your research, experiences, and goals. Stay flexible and open to new information as you move closer to deciding.

2. Seek mentorship. Connect with experienced entrepreneurs and business professionals. Many retired entrepreneurs will gladly spend time with prospective business owners and give valuable guidance.

3. Use networking opportunities: Join industry groups, attend seminars, and take part in networking events to gain insights and advice.

4. Attend workshops and courses: Enroll in entrepreneurship courses, workshops, and webinars to build your knowledge and skills.

5. Attend trade shows and exhibitions: These events can be a powerful tool for networking, learning about industry trends, and discovering new opportunities.

6. Consider trial runs or part-time ventures: Start a small-scale or part-time version of your business idea to test its viability and gather real-world experience without significant risk.

Chapter 5
Types of Businesses – Unique Characteristics

"Even if you are on the right track, you'll get run over if you just sit there" – Will Rodgers

In the previous chapters, we explored the primary business classifications. Now, it's time to discuss a third group, namely those with unique characteristics.

Overview

In this chapter we will explore three types of businesses with unique characteristics. These businesses fit within the legal structures and core business sectors discussed earlier, but they stand out due to their distinct nature. We will examine a franchise, a lifestyle business, and a non-profit organization. Each of these business types offers different opportunities and challenges, making them worthy of separate discussion. By understanding these unique characteristics, you will gain insights into diverse business models that might align with your goals and values.

Franchise

A franchise is a business model that allows individuals to own and operate their own branch of an established company. In this arrangement, the franchisor (the original business) grants the franchisee (the individual owner) the right to use its trademark, trade name, and business systems. This setup provides the franchisee with the advantage of operating under a recognized brand while following a proven business model.

The concept of franchising dates to the mid-19th century. The very first franchise is considered to be the Singer Sewing Machine Company, which started its franchise operations in the 1850s. While Singer is no longer in the franchise business, its pioneering model set the stage for modern franchising. Today, the most recognized franchise brand in the world is McDonald's. With over 38,000 franchisees operating in more than 100 countries, McDonald's boasts annual sales exceeding $21 billion[1].

Franchises typically exhibit strict adherence to the franchisor's established guidelines and operational standards. This ensures uniformity across all franchise locations, maintaining brand integrity and customer expectations. Franchisees must follow specific procedures for product preparation, service delivery, and marketing, which distinguishes franchising from independent business ownership. This rigid structure helps uphold the brand's reputation and provides customers with a consistent experience, regardless of location.

Franchises operate in all three core business sectors discussed earlier: retail, service, and manufacturing. According to the

---

1. Source: McDonald's 2023 Annual Report.

International Franchise Association, approximately 50% of franchises operate in the retail industry, 40% in services, and the remaining 10% in manufacturing[2] .

In the retail sector, Subway is a well-known franchise with thousands of outlets worldwide. In the service sector, notable franchises include Anytime Fitness and H&R Block. In the manufacturing sector, Ben & Jerry's stands out as a recognizable franchise brand, although it could be argued that their franchisees are mostly retailers.

Pros of a Franchise

There are several advantages to starting a franchise.

One of the primary benefits is the established brand recognition, which can attract customers more quickly than a new, unknown business.

The franchisor's proven operating system reduces the trial and error typically associated with starting a business, increasing the chances of success.

Franchisors also provide extensive support and training, helping franchisees navigate the complexities of business operations.

Additionally, ongoing marketing efforts by the franchisor help maintain brand visibility and drive customer traffic to franchise locations.

Other advantages include access to bulk purchasing, which can lower operational costs, and the ability to leverage the franchisor's industry expertise and innovation.

---

2. Source: IFA 2023 Report

Cons of a Franchise

However, there are also drawbacks to franchising.

One of the major cons is the high startup cost, which can include the initial franchise fee, equipment, inventory, and real estate expenses.

Franchisees often have little to no control over the business model, as they must adhere to the franchisor's established systems and procedures. This lack of autonomy can be frustrating for entrepreneurs who prefer to innovate and customize their operations.

Additionally, franchisees must pay ongoing royalties and marketing contributions, which can eat into profits. They may also have to participate in forced upgrades or remodels mandated by the franchisor, incurring additional costs.

Lastly, disputes with the franchisor can arise, particularly if the franchisee feels unsupported or constrained by the franchisor's policies.

Despite these challenges, many first-time entrepreneurs are drawn to franchising due to the reduced risk and support provided. According to a survey by Franchise Direct, approximately 25% of first-time entrepreneurs choose to start with a franchise (source: Franchise Direct 2023 Survey). This statistic highlights the appeal of franchising as a viable entry point into business ownership, offering a blend of independence and support that can be particularly attractive to newcomers.

As the age-old saying goes: "You are in business for yourself, but not by yourself."

Lifestyle Business

A lifestyle business is designed to support the owner's interests and lifestyle rather than maximizing profits. The term was coined in the 1980s to describe businesses that prioritize the entrepreneur's quality of life over aggressive growth and expansion. The first known use of the phrase can be traced back to the early entrepreneurial movements that emphasized personal satisfaction and work-life balance.

Pros of a Lifestyle Business

One of the primary advantages of a lifestyle business is the potential for a harmonious work-life balance. Entrepreneurs can set flexible working hours that fit their schedules, allowing them to prioritize family, hobbies, and other interests. This flexibility often leads to higher personal fulfillment as the business aligns with the owner's passions and values.

Unlike traditional businesses, the primary goal of a lifestyle business is self-fulfillment rather than profit maximization. This attitude fosters a more relaxed and enjoyable work environment, reducing stress and burnout.

Cons of a Lifestyle Business

However, lifestyle businesses also have their drawbacks. One significant limitation is the potential for growth. Since the primary focus is on supporting a particular lifestyle, scaling the business might not be a priority, which can cap its overall growth potential.

Additionally, income variability can be a challenge, as lifestyle businesses might not generate consistent revenue streams, leading to financial uncertainty.

Over time, the non-growth nature of the business can become monotonous, potentially reducing the initial excitement and passion that drove the entrepreneur to start the business.

Lifestyle Entrepreneurs

The typical profile of entrepreneurs who start or buy a lifestyle business often includes individuals seeking a change from the traditional corporate environment. These entrepreneurs can be of any gender, though there tends to be a higher representation of women. They are often in their 30s to 50s, at a stage in life where personal fulfillment and flexible working arrangements become more important.

Many have personal circumstances that demand a flexible schedule, such as caring for children or elderly family members. This demographic group values the autonomy and control that a lifestyle business offers, aligning their work with their personal goals and responsibilities.

One of the most interesting ways that lifestyle businesses come about is when hobbies or passions are turned into businesses. Entrepreneurs still do what they love, but in a more formalized business manner that can contribute handsomely to the household budget, if not in its entirety.

Non-Profit Organization

As a general definition, a non-profit organization (NPO) is an entity set up to serve a public or social cause without the primary goal of making profits for its owners. Any surplus revenue is reinvested into the organization rather than distributed to owners or shareholders.

In the USA, common legal structures for NPOs include 501(c)(3) organizations, charitable trusts, and foundations. These structures are designed to support the organization's mission while providing certain legal and tax benefits. It's worth noting that 501(c)(4) and other 501(c) designations also exist for nonprofits with different goals, such as social welfare organizations.

In the UK, the standard legal structures for NPOs include charitable incorporated organizations (CIOs), charitable trusts, and charitable companies limited by guarantee. The Charity Commission regulates these entities and provides tax benefits similar to those in the US for 501(c)(3) organizations. However, in the UK, the distinction between different types of charitable organizations is less formalized than the US system of 501(c) categories.

In Canada, NPOs are typically structured as registered charities or nonprofit organizations (NPOs) under federal and provincial regulations. Registered charities, like US 501(c)(3) organizations, enjoy tax benefits and can issue tax receipts for donations, while NPOs promote social causes but do not have the same tax advantages.

NPO Versus NGO

Very generally, the main difference between an NPO and a Non-Governmental Organization (NGO) lies in their scope of work and focus:

An NPO is a broad term for any organization that operates for a social, public, or community cause without the goal of generating profit for its owners or shareholders. Their primary focus is on serving a specific cause or community need.

An NGO is a type of nonprofit organization that typically works on a broader scale, often focusing on international issues like humanitarian aid, environmental protection, and human rights. NGOs usually operate independently of governments, although they may work with government agencies.

Just for a smile: while all NGOs are NPOs, not all NPOs are NGOs.

Why is an NPO Included Here?

Despite the name, NPOs can indeed engage in profitable activities. However, the critical distinction is that any profit generated must be reinvested into the organization's mission rather than distributed to owners or shareholders. This model allows NPOs to sustain and expand their operations while keeping their commitment to their social or public causes.

Including NPOs in this discussion highlights that some entrepreneurs are motivated by a desire to help others rather than seeking personal financial gain. These individuals often find fulfillment in applying their skills and talents to make a positive impact on society. While they receive a salary for their work, the primary reward is the satisfaction of contributing to a greater good.

Pros of an NPO

There are several advantages to running an NPO. One significant benefit is the tax-exempt status that many NPOs enjoy, which allows them to allocate more resources toward their mission rather than paying taxes.

NPOs often receive substantial public support through donations, grants, and volunteer efforts. This support can provide a stable source of funding and help amplify the organization's impact.

Cons of an NPO

Strict regulations govern their operations, requiring compliance with various reporting and operational standards. This regulatory environment can be complex and time-consuming, needing dedicated administrative resources.

Funding can also be a significant challenge, as NPOs often rely on donations and grants, which can be unpredictable and competitive to secure. This dependency on external funding sources can create financial instability and limit the organization's ability to plan long-term projects.

Chapter Recap

We delved into the specifics of franchises, highlighting their unique operational model and benefits. We examined lifestyle businesses, emphasizing their focus on personal fulfillment and work-life balance. Finally, we discussed NPOs.

This chapter provided a broad understanding of these diverse business types, aiding aspiring entrepreneurs in deciding which business model best aligns with their goals and values.

In the next chapter, we will look at the essential steps ahead. This will include self-assessment as well as planning and research, which will help you on your journey towards finally deciding whether to start your dream business or not.

Action Plan

Since this chapter was a continuation of the discussion on business types, the action plan of Chapter 4 can be followed.

Chapter 6
Essential Steps Ahead

"Before you are a leader, success is all about growing yourself. When you become a leader, success is all about growing others" — Jack Welch

Overview

In the previous chapters, we covered various aspects that you must consider before starting a business. This chapter continues in the same vein, focusing on the most critical steps ahead.

These steps will help you determine whether you are ready to embark on this journey and whether the business opportunity is viable. We will explore three key areas: self-assessment, market research, and creating a business plan.

Self-assessment will help you gauge your readiness by evaluating your personal circumstances, business acumen, and financial readiness. Market research will provide crucial insights into your target market, competition, and industry trends, enabling you to make informed decisions. Finally, a well-crafted business plan will not only outline your business goals, strategies, and financial projections but also answer the crucial question: Is this business opportunity viable?

This chapter will give you an overview of these steps, setting the stage for making an informed decision about starting your business.

Self-Assessment

Self-assessment is a process of introspection and evaluation where individuals analyze their skills, strengths, weaknesses, and readiness for a particular task or journey.

Self-assessment helps potential entrepreneurs determine whether they are prepared for the challenges and responsibilities of running a business. This evaluation not only aids in understanding one's readiness but can also help identify the type of business that may be most suitable.

Emotional Readiness

Emotional readiness is crucial when considering starting a business. It involves evaluating your emotional resilience, stress management skills, and ability to manage uncertainty.

Starting a business can be stressful and unpredictable, requiring long hours and unwavering commitment. Assess whether you can maintain motivation and positivity even when faced with setbacks. Consider your ability to handle pressure, manage stress, and stay focused on long-term goals.

Reflect on your past experiences in managing stress and overcoming challenges. Are you adaptable and able to keep a clear head in tricky situations? Your emotional state will significantly affect your decision-making and leadership abilities.

Personal and Family Support System

Having a robust personal and family support system is essential when starting a business. This support system includes family members, friends, and mentors who can provide emotional backing, advice, and practical assistance.

Evaluate your current support network. Are your family members supportive of your entrepreneurial aspirations? Do you have friends or mentors who can offer guidance and encouragement?

It's important to discuss your plans with those close to you, as their support can be invaluable during tough times. Assess how starting a business might affect your personal life and relationships. Consider whether you have people around you who understand the demands of entrepreneurship and are willing to support you through the highs and lows.

Business Acumen

Business acumen refers to the ability to understand and deal with various business situations. It encompasses a range of skills, including strategic thinking, financial literacy, and market awareness.

To assess your business acumen, reflect on your past experiences and knowledge. Have you had any exposure to business management, either through education or work experience? Are you comfortable with financial concepts, such as costing, pricing, and financial analysis?

Consider your strategic thinking abilities. Can you develop and execute business strategies effectively? To enhance your skills, it may be helpful to take business courses or seek mentorship from experienced entrepreneurs. Being honest about your current level of business acumen will help you identify areas for improvement and prepare you for the challenges ahead.

Financial Readiness

Financial readiness is a critical aspect of starting a business. It involves assessing your financial stability and understanding the financial demands of starting and running a business.

Evaluate your personal financial situation. Do you have savings that can support you during the first stages of your business when income might be low?

Are you aware of the costs involved in starting your business, such as initial investment, working capital, and potential financial risks? Consider your ability to manage personal finances and make sound financial decisions.

It's important to have a clear understanding of your financial standing and plan accordingly.

The Importance of Critical Self-Assessment

Critical self-assessment is vital in figuring out your readiness to start a business. It provides an honest evaluation of your strengths and weaknesses, helping you make informed decisions.

Use the outcomes of your self-assessment positively to learn and improve. Identify areas where you need growth and seek out resources or training to enhance your skills. Understanding your current readiness allows you to address any gaps and prepare yourself adequately.

This process is not about discouraging you but empowering you with the knowledge and tools to succeed. By being honest with yourself and taking proactive steps to improve, you increase your chances of making the right decision and then building a successful and sustainable business.

Market Research

Moving our attention towards the business opportunity, market research is the next critical step.

Market research is the process of gathering, analyzing, and interpreting information about a market, including information about the target audience, competitors, and the industry. The purpose of market research is to understand the feasibility of your business idea, identify potential opportunities and threats, and make informed decisions based on data rather than assumptions.

Market research can vary significantly in scope and scale. Large corporations might spend millions of dollars on extensive research conducted over several months by teams of professionals. This might include surveys, focus groups, and detailed data analysis.

On the other end of the spectrum, a small business or first-time entrepreneur might conduct market research through more accessible methods, such as online surveys, desktop research, and informal interviews with potential customers.

For small businesses and first-time entrepreneurs, achieving a minimum outcome from market research involves understanding the basics: identifying your target market, analyzing competitors, and assessing market demand.

By far, the most important aspect is having a clear idea of who your potential customers are. Consider factors such as age, gender, income level, and buying habits. Use online tools like Google

Trends, social media analytics, and industry reports to gather information about your target audience. Additionally, conducting surveys or interviews can offer valuable insights into customer preferences and needs.

Analyzing competitors is another essential part of market research. Find out who your main competitors are, what products or services they offer, and what strategies they use to attract customers. This can help you understand the competitive landscape and identify gaps or opportunities in the market. Tools like SWOT analysis (Strengths, Weaknesses, Opportunities, and Threats) can be useful in organizing this information and developing your competitive strategy.

Assessing market demand is difficult but essential for figuring out the viability of your business idea. This involves estimating the potential size of your market and understanding the trends that could affect your business. Look at industry reports, market forecasts, and economic indicators to get a sense of the market's growth potential. Online tools like Statista, IBISWorld, and government databases can provide valuable data for this analysis.

Let's consider a practical example of applying market research. Imagine you plan to open a café in a small town. Through market research, you find that most residents prefer organic and locally sourced products. You also discover that there is only one other café in town, which does not offer organic options. Based on this information, you decide to focus on organic and locally sourced food and beverages. This unique selling proposition can help you attract health-conscious customers and differentiate your business from the competition.

A real-life example of market research prompting a change for the better is the story of Warby Parker, the eyewear company. Initially, the founders planned to sell their products exclusively online. However, through market research, they discovered that many customers preferred trying on glasses before buying. This insight led them to open brick-and-mortar stores, which significantly boosted their sales and customer satisfaction. By listening to their market and adapting their strategy, Warby Parker was able to meet customer needs better and grow their business.

Business Plan

A business plan is a detailed document that outlines your business goals, strategies, target market, financial projections, and operational plans. It serves as a roadmap for your business, guiding you from the initial idea to successful implementation and growth.

The creation of a business plan follows the market research phase. This sequence is crucial because the insights gained from market research inform the business plan, ensuring it is grounded in real-world data and market realities.

A business plan is a multifaceted subject, so much so that an entire book in this series will be devoted to it. The purpose of this discussion is to highlight its importance, briefly discuss its main parts, and prepare you for the next steps in your entrepreneurial journey.

A well-crafted business plan serves three purposes: it helps determine the viability of your business idea, acts as a blueprint for implementation, and is essential for securing financing from investors or lenders.

The main parts of a business plan include:

1. Executive Summary: This section provides a concise overview of your business, summarizing the key points of the entire plan.

2. Business Description: Here, you outline the nature of your business, the market needs it aims to fulfill, and the unique value proposition it offers. This section should give a clear picture of what your business is about and why it is needed.

3. Market Analysis: Based on your market research, this section delves into the details of your target market, including size, demographics, trends, and the competitive landscape. It should demonstrate a thorough understanding of the market environment.

4. Organization and Management: This part describes your business's organizational structure, including details about the ownership, management team, and board of directors, if applicable. It highlights the expertise and experience of those running the business.

5. Product or Service: In this section, you detail the products or services your business offers. Explain the benefits, lifecycle, and the research and development activities involved.

6. Marketing and Sales: This section outlines how you plan to attract and retain customers. It includes your marketing strategy, sales tactics, and the channels you will use to reach your target audience.

7. Funding Request: If you are seeking financing, this section specifies your funding requirements, potential future funding needs, and how you plan to use the funds.

8. Financial Projections: This critical section includes income statements, cash flow statements, and balance sheets. These projections provide a financial forecast for your business and demonstrate its potential for profitability.

9. Appendices: The appendices contain any additional information that supports your business plan, such as resumes, legal documents, and product images.

The result of a well-prepared business plan is a comprehensive document that provides a clear path forward. It enables you to assess the feasibility of your business idea, plan for growth, and communicate your vision to potential investors and stakeholders. With a solid business plan, you are better equipped to navigate the challenges of starting and growing your business, making informed decisions every step of the way.

Chapter Recap

In this chapter, we explored the critical steps ahead.

We began with self-assessment, emphasizing the importance of evaluating emotional readiness, personal and family support systems, business acumen, and financial preparedness. This introspection helps decide if you are ready to embark on the entrepreneurial journey.

Next, we delved into market research, highlighting its role in understanding your target market, competitors, and overall market. We explained how market research can range from extensive corporate studies to simpler methods suitable for small businesses and first-time entrepreneurs.

Finally, we discussed the business plan, detailing its main components and stressing its importance in determining business viability, providing a blueprint for implementation, and securing financing. The business plan follows market research, ensuring it is data-driven and realistic.

In the next chapter, we will examine interesting case studies, offering practical insights and lessons from real-life businesses.

Action Plan

Refer to the section on Self-assessment, and take time to execute the proposed actions for each of the following:

1. Emotional readiness

2. Personal and family support system

3. Business acumen

4. Financial readiness

Make notes of your insights and results. Use this as a guide for further learning and improvement.

Chapter 7
Case Studies

"Success is not final, failure is not fatal: it is the courage to continue that counts" — Winston Churchill

Overview

In this chapter, we delve into real-world examples to illustrate the practical applications of the concepts discussed in earlier chapters.

By examining the journeys of two businesses, we can see how theoretical knowledge translates into actionable strategies. These case studies provide a tangible connection to the challenges explored earlier.

In the first case study, we will examine a retail store with low profit margins, high overhead costs, and minimal use of technology. The second study will focus on a brick-and-mortar retail store that started manufacturing its core product.

To protect the privacy of the entrepreneurs involved, names and identifying details have been changed.

These stories highlight the resilience and creativity needed to succeed in the competitive business world. They also offer the sobering lesson that business success is not guaranteed by enthusiasm alone.

Case Study 1: The Transformation of Trendy Treasures Retail Store

Introduction

Trendy Treasures is a retail store located in a bustling urban area that Alex Turner founded in 2018. With a background in fashion and retail, Alex was passionate about curating a unique collection of clothing, accessories, and home décor items. Despite his enthusiasm, Alex soon faced several significant challenges that threatened the survival of his business.

Background

Alex's motivation for starting Trendy Treasures stemmed from his love for fashion and desire to offer customers unique, high-quality products. He invested his savings into the business, leased a prime location, and stocked the store with carefully selected items. However, Alex's excitement quickly turned to anxiety as he faced low profit margins, high overhead costs, minimal use of technology, and slow-moving inventory.

Challenges and Obstacles

Low Profit Margins: Despite good foot traffic, Alex noticed that his profit margins could have been much higher. The high cost of goods sold, coupled with competitive pricing, left little room for profit.

High Overhead Costs: Trendy Treasures' prime location came with a hefty price tag. Rent, utilities, and staffing costs ate into the already thin profit margins, making it difficult to stay afloat.

Minimal Use of Technology: Alex was using manual methods for inventory management, sales tracking, and customer engagement. This lack of technology integration led to inefficiencies and missed opportunities for growth.

Slow-Moving Inventory: Some of the products in the store moved extremely slowly, tying up capital and space that could be used for more popular items.

Improving Profit Margins

Alex decided to diversify his product range to include higher-margin items. He introduced a line of exclusive, high-quality accessories and home décor pieces that could be sold at a premium price. Additionally, Alex negotiated better terms with suppliers, securing bulk purchase discounts and reducing the cost of goods sold.

Timeline: This strategy took about six months to implement as Alex needed time to find new suppliers, negotiate terms, and introduce new products.

Investment: Minimal financial investment was needed as the focus was on negotiation and strategic purchasing.

Results: Within a year, Alex saw a 15% increase in profit margins, significantly improving the store's financial health.

Reducing Overhead Costs

To tackle high overhead costs, Alex renegotiated his lease, securing a longer-term agreement with a lower monthly rent. He also implemented energy-saving measures to cut utility costs and streamlined staffing by introducing flexible, part-time shifts.

Timeline: The lease renegotiation took three months, while the energy-saving measures and staffing adjustments were rolled out over six months.

Investment: The investment included minor expenses for energy-efficient lighting systems.

Results: These changes resulted in an 11% reduction in monthly overhead costs within a year, easing the business's financial burden.

Integrating Technology

Recognizing the need for technology, Alex invested in a comprehensive retail management system. This system automated inventory management, sales tracking, and customer relationship management (CRM). He also launched an online store to expand his reach beyond the local area.

Timeline: The technology integration took about nine months, including research, system implementation, and staff training.

Investment: The initial investment for the retail management system and website development was around $10,000 at the time.

Results: The store experienced an immediate improvement in efficiency, an almost 23% boost in revenue from online sales, and improved customer satisfaction due to better inventory management and personalized marketing efforts.

Addressing Slow-Moving Inventory

To address slow-moving inventory, Alex conducted a thorough analysis to identify underperforming products. He held promotional sales and offered discounts to clear out old stock. Alex adopted a data-driven approach to inventory management, using sales data to make informed purchasing decisions.

Timeline: The promotional sales and clearance events were executed over three months, while the data-driven inventory approach was an ongoing process.

Investment: Minimal investment was needed, mainly in promotional activities and marketing.

Results: Within six months, Alex successfully cleared out 80% of the slow-moving inventory, freeing up capital and space for more popular items, which led to a further 8% increase in overall sales.

Conclusion

Through strategic product diversification, cost reduction, technology integration, and efficient inventory management, Alex Turner transformed Trendy Treasures into a thriving retail business. By addressing each challenge with practical, implementable steps, Alex not only overcame the initial hurdles but also set the stage for steady growth.

The store's success story serves as an inspiration for prospective entrepreneurs, proving that with the right strategies and determination, it's possible to turn around a struggling business and achieve sustainable success.

Quotes

"Implementing technology was a game-changer for us," Alex reflects. "It not only streamlined our operations but opened new revenue streams through online sales. Looking back, it's clear that these investments were crucial for our survival and growth."

Case Study 2: The rise and fall of Magic Frames

The story of Magic Frames began with high hopes and great promise in the heart of a bustling city.

Driven by poverty and a lack of prospects, Daniel Harris, a high-energy entrepreneur, discovered a source of cheap but quality oil-on-canvas paintings. With determination, he sold these paintings door to door, traveling by foot. This first venture was so successful that Daniel soon bought a panel van, using it as a mobile gallery to sell his artwork.

As his client base grew, many began asking about framing options. Seizing this opportunity, Daniel opened a physical store named Magic Frames, where he sold paintings and offered framing services. Initially, the business was a roaring success with high sales, substantial profit margins, and relatively low overheads.

But soon, a series of poor decisions and personal failings led to its downfall.

Early Success and Expansion

Daniel's business acumen shone brightly in the early days. He identified a niche market and capitalized on it, quickly transitioning from door-to-door sales to a bustling store. Magic Frames became known for its quality products and excellent customer service. The framing service added significant value, attracting more customers and boosting profits. Daniel's success seemed unstoppable, and his confidence soared.

Greed and Overconfidence

However, as the business flourished, greed and overconfidence began to cloud Daniel's judgment. Instead of consolidating his success, he wanted more.

He saw an opportunity to manufacture frames himself, believing this would be cheaper than buying them and that he could also sell them to other framers. The idea seemed sound on the surface, but Daniel lacked the necessary manufacturing expertise.

Ignoring the need for proper research and planning, Daniel impulsively ordered ultramodern manufacturing equipment from Italy. He used his savings to pay the deposit to have it manufactured without securing the necessary financing first, naively believing he could raise the funds before the machinery was ready to be shipped.

In his emotional high, he rented a massive warehouse in an industrial area far from his store, intending to house the manufacturing business.

Mounting Problems

The first major issue arose when Daniel struggled to secure financing for the manufacturing equipment. Financiers, sensing his desperation, offered loans with extremely high interest rates.

Faced with the prospect of losing his deposit, Daniel accepted the onerous terms.

He underestimated the complexity of the manufacturing process, assuming he could simply hire trained people. However, suitably skilled workers were scarce and far more expensive than he expected.

To save money, Daniel decided against paying the manufacturer to commission the machines. This decision proved disastrous, as it took months to get even the first phase of the operation working. It was a year before the first completed products left the factory, by which time all available capital had been exhausted. His lack of experience and refusal to seek expert advice had created a costly and inefficient setup.

Neglecting the Core Business

As Daniel focused all his time and energy on the factory, he should have paid more attention to his store. The once-thriving Magic Frames began to suffer. Customer service declined, product quality dropped, and sales plummeted. Loyal customers were disappointed, and negative word-of-mouth spread rapidly. The store's revenue, which had once been the backbone of Daniel's success, dwindled.

The financial strain was immense. High-interest loans and operational inefficiencies at the factory drained the business's resources. With no financiers willing to lend more, Daniel's dream began to crumble. The factory's slow start meant there was no income to offset the mounting debts.

The Final Blow

The situation reached a breaking point when the first financier foreclosed on Daniel's loans. With his assets tied up and no way to repay the debts, Magic Frames faced inevitable bankruptcy.

The dream that had once seemed so promising ended in financial ruin.

What Went Wrong

Daniel's downfall resulted from both personal and business missteps. His greed led him to overextend without proper planning, and his overconfidence made him dismissive of advice and resistant to seeking help.

He underestimated the complexities of manufacturing and overestimated his ability to manage it. By neglecting his core business in pursuit of new ventures, he alienated his customer base and destroyed his primary source of revenue.

Solid Business Advice

As the foreclosure proceedings began, the lead financier offered poignant advice: "In business, ambition is necessary, but unchecked greed and poor planning are recipes for disaster. Success requires not only vision but also the wisdom to know your limits and the humility to seek help when needed."

Conclusion

The rise and fall of Magic Frames serve as a cautionary tale for aspiring entrepreneurs. Daniel Harris's story highlights the dangers of overexpansion, the importance of thorough planning, and the need to balance ambition with practical wisdom.

His journey from poverty to success and ultimately to bankruptcy underscores the critical lessons every business owner must learn to achieve sustainable growth. By recognizing and addressing these pitfalls, future entrepreneurs can navigate their paths with greater insight and resilience.

Chapter Recap

In this chapter, we explored two contrasting case studies that offer valuable lessons for aspiring entrepreneurs and new small business owners.

The first case study highlighted the success story of Trendy Treasures, where Alex Turner transformed a struggling retail business into a thriving enterprise.

Key lessons from Alex's journey include the importance of diversifying product ranges to improve profit margins, reducing overhead costs through strategic negotiations, and integrating technology to streamline operations and expand market reach. Alex's ability to identify and address slow-moving inventory also underscored the necessity of data-driven decision-making.

In stark contrast, the story of Magic Frames serves as a cautionary tale.

Daniel Harris's initial success in the retail market was undermined by a series of poor decisions driven by greed and overconfidence. His lack of proper planning and expertise in manufacturing led to financial ruin. Key lessons from Daniel's downfall include the dangers of overexpansion without adequate research and the critical importance of seeking expert advice when venturing into unfamiliar territory. Additionally, neglecting a core business in pursuit of new opportunities can lead to customer dissatisfaction and revenue decline.

Together, these case studies emphasize the balance between ambition and practical wisdom. They highlight the need for careful planning, strategic decision-making, and continuous focus on core business operations to achieve sustainable growth.

Action Plan

From these case studies, list all the challenges and solutions that:

1. Is applicable to your situation, or

2. What you think you need more information on.

Use this list as a guide for further learning and self-improvement.

Chapter 8
Conclusion

"Your work is going to fill a large part of your life, and the only way to be truly satisfied is to do what you believe is great work. And the only way to do great work is to love what you do. If you haven't found it yet, keep looking. Don't settle. As with all matters of the heart, you'll know when you find it" — Steve Jobs

Recap of Key Topics

The purpose of this book is to guide aspiring entrepreneurs and new small business owners through the essential aspects of starting and running a business.

We aim to give practical advice, real-life examples, and actionable strategies to help you navigate the complexities of the entrepreneurial journey. We strive to make the decision to go into business easier.

Introduction set the stage by explaining the book's purpose. It highlighted the importance of informed decision-making and continuous learning in entrepreneurship.

Chapter 1: Reasons to Start a Business delved into the motivations behind entrepreneurship. It explored personal, professional, and financial reasons, helping readers understand their driving factors. The chapter also discussed the potential rewards and challenges of starting a business.

Chapter 2: Key Business Components to Consider provided insights into crucial elements like capital, labor, technology, and operations. Understanding these components is vital for making informed decisions about your business set-up and growth strategies.

Chapter 3 to 5: Types of Businesses discussed various legal structures and core business sectors. It covered sole proprietorships, partnerships, LLCs, and corporations, outlining their pros and cons. The chapters also explored different business sectors, including retail, service, manufacturing, and e-commerce. Special business types like franchises, lifestyle businesses, and non-profits were examined for their unique characteristics.

Chapter 6: Important Steps Ahead focused on self-assessment, market research, and creating a business plan. It emphasized the importance of evaluating readiness, understanding your target market, and crafting a detailed plan to ensure business viability.

Chapter 7: Case Studies offered practical lessons from real-world business scenarios. It highlighted successful strategies and common pitfalls through detailed examples, reinforcing the book's theoretical concepts.

By revisiting these key points, you can better prepare for your entrepreneurial journey.

Final Thoughts and Encouragement

For prospective entrepreneurs: I have authored this book not to encourage you to start a business but to guide you in making an informed decision about starting one.

The decision you make is personal, and no one can call it right or wrong if it is based on a solid foundation of knowledge. My goal is to provide you with the information and insights you need to weigh the pros and cons, understand the challenges, and evaluate your readiness. Whether you decide to take the plunge or not, making a well-informed choice is crucial.

For new small business owners: Congratulations on starting a business! I deeply appreciate the courage it takes to start and run a business.

I structured this book to help you identify areas for improvement and encourage you to pursue lifelong learning. Business ownership is a continuous journey of growth and adaptation. By staying informed and seeking opportunities for development, you can navigate the challenges and achieve your goals.

Starting a business is like walking through a foggy morning. You can only see fifty meters ahead, but how do you see the next fifty? By walking the fifty meters you can see. If you do that, the next fifty will appear. Contemplating or starting a business venture is often the same. You will sometimes only see a part of the road ahead. But take courage and do what you can, and the next steps will reveal themselves.

From our personal lives to our business endeavors, we cannot wait until we know everything we need to know. We must go ahead and do the best we can with what we know. Then keep learning and studying, and as we know better, we can do better.

Your journey in business will be filled with unknowns, but with determination and continuous learning, you can overcome obstacles and find success.

Next Steps

For prospective entrepreneurs, the next steps involve critically evaluating your readiness to start a business. Begin with a thorough self-assessment to gauge your emotional, financial, and business acumen. Create a plan to build the body of knowledge you will require to make that final decision.

For new small business owners, focus on refining your business operations. Review your business plan regularly and adjust it as necessary. Continuously seek ways to improve your products or services, streamline processes, and enhance customer satisfaction. Lifelong learning is critical—attend workshops, read industry-related books, and network with other business owners to stay updated on best practices and trends.

I have included an action plan at the end of each chapter to guide you through these steps. Appendix A combines all these action plans, offering a comprehensive guide. Appendix B provides links to recommended reading, and Appendix C has a glossary of terms and concepts used in this book to help you understand and apply the information effectively.

By following these next steps and using the resources provided in the appendices, you are walking the fifty meters that you can see!

Appendix A: Action plan

Combining the various chapters' plans, you can use this plan to help you plot your way.

 This QR code is clickable and will take you to our website to download the Action Plan below or scan the code from your phone.

Chapter 1: Reasons to Go into Business

Entrepreneurs who are already in business can take a little time to ensure that their reasons for starting the business are aligned with their personal goals. If not, now is an excellent time to clarify this.

For prospective entrepreneurs still contemplating the idea of going into business, I can suggest the following:

1. Carefully consider the reasons we discussed in this chapter.

2. Write down the reason that resonates with you. If there are more than one, jot them down too.

3. Take time to decide whether these reasons are how you truly feel and how you think about your future. Adjust your list - the more clearly you describe this, the better.

4. Once you clearly understand your reason(s) for going into business, you can work on understanding the potential disadvantages. This understanding will positively impact your planning.

For both groups, I suggest you share your thoughts with family and friends, especially that one person who will likely be your most significant pillar of support, your spouse.Also, network with entrepreneurs that are already doing what you intend to do. Learn from other people's experiences and, importantly, learn from success.

Chapter 2: Key Business Components to Consider

Both existing and prospective entrepreneurs will benefit from spending time sharpening their understanding of the components most relevant to their business or likely to influence them in the future.

Existing entrepreneurs

1. List all the components that are relevant to your business, including the specific risks.

2. Make a list of specific aspects you need to research or learn to mitigate those risks.

3. Start crafting an implementation plan, and don't wait until you have all the answers; implement as and when you find

a solution. Small, immediate gains can be a game changer.

Prospective entrepreneurs

1. List those business components you want to avoid altogether.

2. Separately, list those components that you are comfortable with, have knowledge about, and that you can manage.

3. Measure all business opportunities against these two lists to find a business that fits your preferences and your goals.

Chapter 3: Legal Structure

If you have not yet decided on a legal structure for your business, or you want to make changes, I can suggest the following plan:

1. Decide which legal structure best suits your plans.

2. Make a list of specific questions you have about the structure.

3. Make a list of sources (for example, books, websites, or a business coach) available that can provide the required information.

Chapter 4, 5: Core Business Sector, Unique Characteristics

If you already know what type of business you want to start or already are in business, congratulations!If undecided, there are many sources available to get your mind racing:

1. Self-evaluation. Reflect on what you are passionate about and what you want to achieve. Consider how each business model aligns with your personal and professional aspirations. Make a list of your strong points, areas of expertise, preferences, interests, and passions. On the negative side, make a list of things, situations, and environments that you are not interested in. Periodically review your research, experiences, and goals. Stay flexible and open to new information as you move closer to deciding.

2. Seek mentorship. Connect with experienced entrepreneurs and business professionals. Many retired entrepreneurs will gladly spend time with prospective business owners and give valuable guidance.

3. Use networking opportunities: Join industry groups, attend seminars, and take part in networking events to gain insights and advice.

4. Attend workshops and courses: Enroll in entrepreneurship courses, workshops, and webinars to build your knowledge and skills.

5. Attend trade shows and exhibitions: These events can be a powerful tool for networking, learning about industry trends, and discovering new opportunities.

6. Consider trial runs or part-time ventures: Start a small-scale or part-time version of your business idea to test its viability and gather real-world experience without significant risk.

Chapter 6: Self-Assessment

Refer to the section on Self-Assessment, and take time to execute the proposed actions for each of the following:

> 1. Emotional readiness
>
> 2. Personal and family support system
>
> 3. Business acumen
>
> 4. Financial readiness

Make notes of your insights and results. Use this as a guide for further learning and improvement.

Chapter 7: Case Studies

From these case studies, list all the challenges and solutions that:

> 1. Are applicable to your situation, or
>
> 2. What you think you need more information on.

Use this list as a guide for further learning and self-improvement.

Appendix B: Resources

I can recommend the following books[1] which explore entrepreneurship from various perspectives, including motivations, challenges, and opportunities:

"Start with Why" by Simon Sinek

This book focuses on the concept that people are driven by a deeper purpose or belief in why they do what they do. It's excellent for understanding the emotional and psychological motivations behind starting a business.

"The E-Myth Revisited" by Michael E. Gerber

The author explains why many small businesses fail and offers insights into the mindsets and reasons people choose to become entrepreneurs. This book is particularly valuable for understanding the balance between passion and practicality in business.

---

1. As an Amazon Associate, the publisher earns from qualifying purchases.

"Drive: The Surprising Truth About What Motivates Us" by Daniel H. Pink

The book delves into human motivation, offering insights into why people choose specific paths, including entrepreneurship. It highlights the role of autonomy, mastery, and purpose in driving people to start their businesses.

Appendix C: Glossary

These definitions are concise and intended for quick reference, rather than comprehensive explanations as found in formal investment or business finance dictionaries.

Balance Sheet: A financial statement that summarizes a company's assets, liabilities, and shareholders' equity at a specific point in time.

Barrier to Entry: Factors that prevent or hinder new companies from entering a particular market, such as high startup costs, regulatory requirements, or strong brand loyalty of existing firms.

Brand: A unique identifier for a company's products or services, encompassing its name, logo, design, and overall reputation.

Breakeven: The point at which total revenues equal total costs, resulting in neither profit nor loss.

Business Culture: The shared values, beliefs, and practices within a company that shape its interactions and operations.

Business Model: A plan or strategy a company uses to generate revenue and make a profit from its operations.

Business Strategy: A plan of action designed to achieve specific business objectives, typically involving long-term goals and competitive positioning.

Cash Flow Statement: A financial document that provides an overview of cash inflows and outflows over a period and highlights the company's liquidity.

Competitive Strategy: Approaches a company takes to gain an advantage over its competitors, such as cost leadership, differentiation, or focusing on a niche market.

Compliance: Adherence to laws, regulations, guidelines, and specifications relevant to a business or industry.

Consumer Behavior: The study of how individuals or groups select, purchase, use, and dispose of goods, services, and experiences.

Cost of Goods Sold (COGS): The direct costs attributable to the production of the goods sold by a company, including materials and labor.

Costing: The process of calculating the total costs associated with producing a product or providing a service.

Customer Experience: The overall perception a customer has of their interactions with a company, from initial contact to post-purchase support.

Customer Relationship Management (CRM): Systems and strategies for managing a company's interactions with current and potential customers.

Debt Capital: Funds borrowed by a business to be paid back with interest, used to finance operations or growth.

Demographics: Statistical data relating to the population and particular groups within it, such as age, gender, income, and education.

Digital Platform: An online framework that allows users to interact, share content, and perform transactions, such as websites or social media networks.

Digital Wallet: An electronic device or online service that allows individuals to make electronic transactions.

Disruptive Technology: Innovations that significantly alter or replace existing technologies or markets, often creating new industries.

Dividend: A portion of a company's earnings distributed to shareholders, typically in cash or additional shares.

Drop Shipping: A retail fulfillment method in which a store doesn't keep the products it sells in stock; instead, it transfers customer orders and shipment details to a third party.

E-commerce: The buying and selling of goods and services over the internet.

Economic Cycles: The natural fluctuation of the economy between periods of expansion and contraction.

Emerging Markets: Economies that are in the process of rapid growth and industrialization, often characterized by improving infrastructure and increasing income levels.

Environmental Impact: The effect that a company's activities have on the natural environment, including factors like pollution and resource depletion.

Equity Capital: Funds raised by a company in exchange for a share of ownership in the business.

Financial Analysis: The evaluation of a company's financial statements and performance to make informed business decisions.

Financial Feasibility: The assessment of a project's or business's ability to generate sufficient revenue to cover costs and produce a profit.

Focus Group: A diverse group of people assembled to participate in a discussion about a product or service to provide feedback.

Franchise: A business model where a franchisor grants a franchisee the right to operate a business using its name, trademark, and system.

Freelance: Working independently rather than being employed by a company, often offering services to multiple clients.

Gross Domestic Product (GDP): The total value of all goods and services produced within a country over a specific period, typically used as an indicator of economic health.

Impulse Buying: The spontaneous and unplanned purchase of goods or services.

Income Statement: A financial statement that shows a company's revenues, expenses, and profits over a specific period.

Industry: A group of companies that operate in the same segment of the economy and provide similar products or services.

Industry Sector: A distinct subset of the economy comprising businesses that share common activities, such as technology, healthcare, or finance.

Influencer: An individual who has the power to affect the purchasing decisions of others due to their authority, knowledge, position, or relationship with their audience.

Initial Investment: The amount of capital required to start a business or project.

Inventory: The goods and materials a business holds for the purpose of resale.

Inventory Management: The process of ordering, storing, and using a company's inventory, including raw materials, components, and finished products.

Labor Intensive: Industries or processes that require a high level of manual labor to produce goods or services.

Market Research: The process of gathering, analyzing, and interpreting information about a market, including data on potential customers and competitors.

Market Saturation: A situation in which a market is fully supplied with a product, making it difficult for new entrants to gain market share.

Market Segmentation: The practice of dividing a broad market into distinct subsets of consumers with common needs or characteristics.

Market Share: The portion of a market controlled by a particular company or product.

Marketing Strategy: A business's overall game plan for reaching prospective consumers and turning them into customers of their products or services.

Mobile App: A software application designed to run on mobile devices such as smartphones and tablets.

Online Platform: A digital space where users can interact, share content, and perform transactions.

Overhead Cost: Ongoing business expenses not directly attributed to creating a product or service, such as rent, utilities, and insurance.

Partnership Agreement: A legal document that outlines the terms and conditions of a business partnership.

Pass-Through Taxation: A tax treatment where business profits are passed directly to the owners' personal income, avoiding corporate income tax.

Payment Gateway: A service that authorizes and processes payments for online and brick-and-mortar businesses.

Personal Liability: The legal responsibility of an individual to repay debts or cover losses, extending to their personal assets.

Pop-up Shop: A temporary retail space that opens for a short period to achieve a particular goal, such as promoting a new product.

Pricing: The process of determining the value that will be charged for a product or service.

Product Life Cycle: The stages a product goes through, from conception and introduction to growth, maturity, and decline.

Product Shelf Life: The length of time a product remains usable, fit for consumption, or saleable.

Profit Margin: The percentage of revenue that exceeds the costs of production and selling expenses, indicating the profitability of a business.

Quality Control: The process of ensuring that products meet specified standards and are free from defects.

Raw Materials: The essential substances used in the production of goods, typically natural resources or agricultural products.

Regulatory: Pertaining to the rules, laws, and guidelines established by government or other authoritative bodies that businesses must follow.

Revenue: The total income generated by the sale of goods or services related to the company's primary operations.

Royalty: A payment made to the owner of a patent, copyright, franchise, or other intellectual property for the use of that property.

Sales Channels: The various pathways through which a product or service is sold to customers, such as retail stores, online marketplaces, and direct sales.

Sales Tactics: The techniques and methods used by salespeople to persuade customers to make a purchase.

Search Engine Optimization (SEO): The practice of increasing the quantity and quality of traffic to a website through organic search engine results.

Spending Patterns: The habits or trends in the way consumers spend their money.

Statutory: Relating to laws or regulations enacted by a legislative body.

Stock Control: The process of managing the supply, storage, and accessibility of items to ensure an adequate supply without excessive oversupply.

Strategic Planning: The process of defining a company's direction and making decisions on allocating resources to pursue this direction.

Strategy: A plan of action designed to achieve long-term or overall aims and objectives.

Supply Chain: The network of all the individuals, organizations, resources, activities, and technology involved in the creation and sale of a product.

Supply Chain Management: The management of the flow of goods and services, including all processes that transform raw materials into final products.

SWOT Analysis: A strategic planning technique used to identify a company's internal strengths and weaknesses, as well as external opportunities and threats.

Target Market: A specific group of consumers identified as the recipients of a particular marketing message or campaign.

Viability: The ability of a business or product to continue to exist or succeed over the long term.

Working Capital: The difference between a company's current assets and current liabilities, representing the liquidity available to a business for day-to-day operations.

Afterword

Thank you for reading!

If you found this book helpful, I'd greatly appreciate it if you could take a moment to leave a review on Amazon. Your feedback not only helps me improve but also assists other readers in finding the right resources. Scan the QR code (or click on it) to share your thoughts.

I appreciate your support!

About the Author

Born in South Africa and now residing in Panama, Charlie Victor has dedicated his life to the world of small business. With a Bachelor of Commerce and a postgraduate degree in Investment Management, he has a solid academic foundation that complements his practical experience. A serial entrepreneur, Charlie has spent his entire career immersed in small business finance, development and management.

After serving as a pilot in the military, he turned his focus to the business world, assisting hundreds of small businesses in their growth journeys. Many of these ventures have flourished into large, profitable enterprises. Before taking early retirement, Charlie co-founded and served as COO of an international SME finance company where he played a pivotal role in establishing and training in-country teams.

With extensive travel experience, much of it work-related, Charlie draws on his extensive experiences to provide practical, actionable advice for prospective entrepreneurs and new small business owners.

About the Publisher

Impisi™ Media is a dynamic publishing company dedicated to creating and distributing high-quality intellectual property, including books, e-books, audiobooks, and journals.

Our content is crafted to inform, inspire, and empower a global audience. Our commitment to innovation and excellence drives us to deliver content that resonates and adds value to our readers and listeners.

Visit our website https://www.impisimedia.com

f   facebook.com/impisimedia

⊙   instagram.com/impisimedia

𝓟   pinterest.com/impisimedia

Also by the Publisher

Small Business Series

Should You Start a Business or Not?
Business Entry: Starting vs Buying

Smart Work-Life Series

Mastering Time for Productivity

www.impisimedia.com

Join the newsletter to receive updates on new releases.

www.ingramcontent.com/pod-product-compliance
Lightning Source LLC
Chambersburg PA
CBHW071703210326
41597CB00017B/2305